Congressional
Research
Service

Iraq: Politics, Governance, and Human Rights

Kenneth Katzman
Specialist in Middle Eastern Affairs

October 2, 2012

Congressional Research Service

7-5700

www.crs.gov

RS21968

CRS Report for Congress ——————————————————

Prepared for Members and Committees of Congress

Summary

Relations among major political factions broke down in late 2011—a development that, when coupled with spillover from increasingly sectarian conflict in Syria, threatens Iraq's stability, its ability to balance its relations with both Tehran and Washington and the achievements of the long U.S. intervention in Iraq. Sunni Arabs, always fearful that Prime Minister Nuri al-Maliki would seek unchallenged power for Shiite factions, accuse him of sidelining high ranking Sunni Arabs from government. Iraq's Kurds have also become increasingly distrustful of Maliki over territorial, political, and economic issues, and are threatening to limit or end their involvement in the central government. The Shiite faction of Moqtada Al Sadr supported the other groups' efforts in mid-2012 to try to oust Maliki, but Iran—a key Maliki ally and supporter—pressed Sadr to discontinue that action, contributing to the failure of the ouster drive. The infighting, coupled with the emboldening of Iraqi Sunni insurgents by the Sunni-led uprising in Syria, has produced increasingly ambitious attacks by Iraqi Sunni insurgent groups, particularly Al Qaeda in Iraq. These attacks are testing the ability of Iraqi security forces and undermining Maliki's reputation as an ensurer of security and stability. The violence is intended to reignite all-out sectarian conflict, but the attacks have failed to spark such broad conflict to date. However, the political rift and the violence have not halted governance or prevented oil export-led growth.

The continuing violence and governmental dysfunctions have called into question the legacy of U.S. involvement in Iraq. In line with the November 2008 bilateral U.S.-Iraq Security Agreement, President Obama announced on October 21, 2011, that U.S. forces would leave Iraq entirely at the end of 2011. Insufficient Iraqi political support caused the Iraqi leadership to turn down a U.S. proposal to retain some U.S. troops after 2011. The proposal was based on U.S. doubts over the ability of Iraqi security forces to preserve the earlier gains and on a U.S. view that a continued troop presence would ensure U.S. influence beyond 2011. About 12,500 U.S. personnel, including contractors, remain in Iraq under State Department authority, but the State Department has assessed that number as too large for the existing missions and a 25% Embassy staffing reduction is planned by the end of 2013.

As U.S. troops completed the withdrawal by December 18, 2011, Administration officials asserted publicly that Iraq's governing and security capacity is sufficient to continue building a stable and democratic Iraq. Iraq's security forces number nearly 700,000 members, increasingly well-armed and well-trained. However, the Administration asserts that the ongoing violence necessitates that Iraq rededicate itself to military cooperation with and assistance from the United States, using State and Defense Department programs. These have included U.S. training for Iraq's security forces through an Office of Security Cooperation—Iraq (OSC-I) and a State Department police development program. To date, these programs have been hampered by Iraqi efforts to emerge from U.S. tutelage: the police training program has withered and OSC-I efforts have been limited by a lack of agreement with Iraq on their legal rights and privileges in Iraq. As of August 2012, in view of the violence, Iraq has requested expedited delivery of U.S. arms as well as joint training.

Other major bilateral issues include Iraq's refusal to call for Iran's ally, Bashar Al Assad of Syria, to yield power amid major unrest. And, Iraq may be cooperating with Iran's efforts to resupply Assad. Others see Iraq trying to reestablish its historic role as a major player in the Arab world, and to do so Iraq has been trying to rebuild relations with Sunni Arab states, particularly Saudi Arabia and Kuwait. Iraq took a large step toward returning to the Arab fold by hosting an Arab League summit on March 27-29, 2012.

Contents

Tables

Contacts

Overview of the Post-Saddam Political Transition

During the 2003-2011 presence of U.S. forces, Iraq completed a transition from the dictatorship of Saddam Hussein to a plural political system in which varying sects and ideological and political factions compete in elections. A series of elections began in 2005, after a one-year occupation period and a subsequent seven-month interim period of Iraqi self-governance. There has been a consensus among Iraqi elites since 2005 to give each community a share of power and prestige to promote cooperation and unity. Still, disputes over the relative claim of each community on power and economic resources permeated almost every issue in Iraq and were never fully resolved. The constant infighting among the major factions over their perceived share of power and resources has interfered with the basic functions of governing and produced popular frustration over a failure of government to deliver services.

Initial Transition and Construction of the Political System

After the fall of Saddam Hussein's regime in April 2003, the United States set up an occupation structure, reportedly based on concerns that immediate sovereignty would favor major factions and not produce democracy. In May 2003, President Bush, reportedly seeking strong leadership in Iraq, named Ambassador L. Paul Bremer to head a "Coalition Provisional Authority" (CPA), which was recognized by the United Nations as an occupation authority. Bremer discontinued a tentative political transition process and instead appointed (July 13, 2003) a non-sovereign Iraqi advisory body, the 25-member "Iraq Governing Council" (IGC). During that year, U.S. and Iraqi negotiators, advised by a wide range of international officials and experts, drafted a "Transitional Administrative Law" (TAL, interim constitution), which became effective on March 4, 2004.[1]

After about one year of occupation, the United States, following a major debate between the CPA and various Iraqi factions over the modalities and rapidity of a resumption of Iraqi sovereignty, handed sovereignty to an appointed Iraqi interim government on June 28, 2004. That date was two days ahead of the TAL-specified date of June 30, 2004, for the handing over of Iraqi sovereignty and the end of the occupation period, which also laid out the elections roadmap discussed below. The interim government was headed by a prime minister, Iyad al-Allawi, leader of the Iraq National Accord, a secular, non-sectarian faction but whose supporters are mostly Sunni Arabs. Allawi is a Shiite Muslim but many INA leaders were Sunnis, and some of them were formerly members of the Baath Party. The president was Sunni tribalist Ghazi al-Yawar.

January 30, 2005, Elections for an Interim Government

Iraqi leaders who rose to prominence after the fall of Saddam Hussein had always assumed that a series of elections would determine the composition of Iraq's new power structure. The beginning of the elections process was set for 2005 to produce a transitional parliament that would supervise writing a new constitution, a public referendum on a new constitution, and then the election of a full term government under that constitution.

In accordance with the dates specified in the TAL, the first post-Saddam election was held on January 30, 2005. The voting was for a 275-seat transitional National Assembly (which formed an

---

[1] Text, in English, is at: http://www.constitution.org/cons/iraq/TAL.html

executive), four-year-term provincial councils in all 18 provinces, and a Kurdistan regional assembly (111 seats). The election for the transitional Assembly was conducted according to the "proportional representation/closed list" election system, in which voters chose among "political entities" (a party, a coalition of parties, or people). A total of 111 entities were on the national ballot, of which 9 were multi-party coalitions.

Still restive over their displacement from power in the 2003 U.S. invasion, Sunni Arabs (20% of the overall population) boycotted, winning only 17 Assembly seats, and only 1 seat on the 51-seat Baghdad provincial council. That council was dominated (28 seats) by representatives of the Islamic Supreme Council of Iraq (ISCI), then led by Abd al-Aziz al-Hakim. (In August 2003, when Abd al-Aziz's brother, Mohammad Baqr al-Hakim, was assassinated in a bombing outside a Najaf mosque, Abd al-Aziz succeeded his brother as ISCI leader. After Abd al-Aziz al-Hakim's death from lung cancer in August 2009, his son Ammar, born in 1971, succeeded him.)

Radical Shiite cleric Moqtada Al Sadr, whose armed faction (the militia operated under the name Mahdi Army) was then at odds with U.S. forces, also boycotted, leaving his faction poorly represented on provincial councils in the Shiite south and in Baghdad. The resulting transitional government placed Shiites and Kurds in the highest positions—Patriotic Union of Kurdistan (PUK) leader Jalal Talabani was president and Da'wa (Shiite party) leader Ibrahim al-Jafari was prime minister. Sunnis were Assembly speaker, deputy president, a deputy prime minister, and six ministers, including defense.

Permanent Constitution[2]

The elected Assembly was to draft a permanent constitution by August 15, 2005, to be put to a referendum by October 15, 2005, subject to veto by a two-thirds majority of voters in any three provinces. On May 10, 2005, a 55-member drafting committee was appointed, but with only two Sunni Arabs (15 Sunnis were later added as full members and 10 as advisors). In August 2005, the talks produced a draft, providing for:

- The three Kurdish-controlled provinces of Dohuk, Irbil, and Sulaymaniyah to constitute a legal "region" administered by the Kurdistan Regional Government (KRG), which would have its own elected president and parliament (Article 113).

- a December 31, 2007, deadline to hold a referendum on whether Kirkuk (Tamim province) would join the Kurdish region (Article 140).

- designation of Islam as "a main source" of legislation.

- all orders of the U.S.-led occupation authority (Coalition Provisional Authority, CPA) to be applicable until amended (Article 126), and a "Federation Council" (Article 62), a second chamber with size and powers to be determined in future law (not adopted to date).

- a 25% electoral goal for women (Article 47).

- families to choose which courts to use for family issues (Article 41); making only primary education mandatory (Article 34).

[2] Text of the Iraqi constitution is at: http://www.washingtonpost.com/wp-dyn/content/article/2005/10/12/AR2005101201450.html.

- having Islamic law experts and civil law judges on the federal supreme court (Article 89). Many Iraqi women opposed this and the previous provisions as giving too much discretion to male family members.

- two or more provinces to join together to form new autonomous "regions"—reaffirmed in passage of an October 2006 law on formation of regions.

- "regions" to organize internal security forces, legitimizing the fielding of the Kurds' *peshmerga* militia (Article 117). This continue a TAL provision.

- the central government to distribute oil and gas revenues from "current fields" in proportion to population, and for regions to have a role in allocating revenues from new energy discoveries (Article 109). Disputes over these concepts continue to hold up passage of national hydrocarbons legislation. Sunnis dominate areas of Iraq that have few proven oil or gas deposits, and favor centralized control of oil revenues, whereas the Kurds want to maintain maximum control of their own burgeoning energy sector.

However, these provisions left many disputes unresolved, particularly the balance between central government and regional and local authority. With this basic question unresolved, Sunnis registered in large numbers (70%-85%) to try to defeat the constitution, prompting a U.S.-mediated agreement (October 11, 2005) providing for a panel to propose amendments within four months after a post-December 15 election government took office (Article 137), to be voted on within another two months (under the same rules as the October 15 referendum). The Sunni provinces of Anbar and Salahuddin (which includes Saddam's home town of Tikrit) had a 97% and 82% "no" vote, respectively, but the constitution was adopted because Nineveh province voted 55% "no," missing the threshold for three provinces to vote "no" by a two-thirds majority.

December 15, 2005, Elections

The December 15, 2005, elections were for a full-term (four-year) national government (also in line with the schedule laid out in the TAL). Under the voting mechanism used for that election, each province contributed a predetermined number of seats to a "Council of Representatives" (COR)—a formula adopted to attract Sunni participation. Of the 275-seat body, 230 seats were allocated this way, with 45 "compensatory" seats for entities that would have won additional seats had the constituency been the whole nation. There were 361 political "entities," including 19 multi-party coalitions, competing in a "closed list" voting system (in which party leaders choose the people who will actually sit in the Assembly). As shown in **Table 5**, voters chose lists representing their sects and regions, and the Shiites and Kurds again emerged dominant. The COR was inaugurated on March 16, 2006, but political infighting caused the Shiite bloc "United Iraqi Alliance" to replace Jafari with another Da'wa figure, Nuri Kamal al-Maliki, as Prime Minister.

On April 22, 2006, the COR approved Talabani to continue as president. His two deputies were Adel Abd al-Mahdi (incumbent) of the Islamic Supreme Council of Iraq (ISCI) and Tariq al-Hashimi, leader of a broad Sunni coalition called the Accord Front ("Tawafuq"—within which Hashimi leads the Iraqi Islamic Party). Another Accord figure, the hardline Mahmoud Mashhadani (National Dialogue Council party), became COR speaker. Maliki won COR approval of a 37-member cabinet (including two deputy prime ministers) on May 20, 2006. Three key slots (Defense, Interior, and National Security) were not filled permanently until June 2006, due to infighting. Of the 37 posts, there were 19 Shiites; 9 Sunnis; 8 Kurds; and 1 Christian. Four were women.

2006-2011: Sectarian Conflict and U.S.-Assisted Reconciliation

The 2005 elections were, at the time, considered successful by the Bush Administration but did not resolve the Sunni-Arab grievances over their diminished positions in the power structure. However, later events suggested that the elections in 2005 might have worsened the violence by exposing and reinforcing the political weakness of the Sunni Arabs. With tensions high, the bombing of a major Shiite shrine within the Sunni-dominated province of Salahuddin in February 2006 set off major sectarian unrest, characterized in part by Sunni insurgent activities against government and U.S. troops, high-casualty suicide and other bombings, and the empowerment of Shiite militia factions to counter the Sunni acts. The sectarian violence was so serious that many experts, by the end of 2006, were considering the U.S. mission as failing, an outcome that an "Iraq Study Group" concluded was a significant possibility absent a major change in U.S. policy.[3]

Benchmarks and a Troop Surge

As assessments of possible overall U.S. policy failure multiplied, in August 2006, the Administration and Iraq agreed on a series of "benchmarks" that, if adopted and implemented, might achieve political reconciliation. Under Section 1314 of a FY2007 supplemental appropriation (P.L. 110-28), "progress" on 18 political and security benchmarks—as assessed in Administration reports due by July 15, 2007, and then September 15, 2007—was required for the United States to provide $1.5 billion in Economic Support Funds (ESF) to Iraq. President Bush exercised the waiver provision. The law also mandated an assessment by the GAO, by September 1, 2007, of Iraqi performance on the benchmarks, as well as an outside assessment of the Iraqi security forces (ISF).

In early 2007, the United States began a "surge" of about 30,000 additional U.S. forces (bringing U.S. troop levels from their 2004-2006 baseline of about 138,000 to about 170,000 at the height of the surge) intended to blunt insurgent momentum and take advantage of growing Sunni Arab rejection of extremist groups. The Administration cited the Iraq Study Group as recommending a temporary surge of troops as well as linking the continued U.S. military presence to Iraqi leaders' commitment to reconciliation. As 2008 progressed, citing the achievement of many of the major Iraqi legislative benchmarks and a dramatic drop in sectarian violence that was attributed to surge, the Bush Administration asserted that political reconciliation was advancing. However, U.S. officials maintained that its extent and durability would depend on the degree of implementation of adopted laws, on further compromises among ethnic groups, and on continued attenuated levels of violence. For Iraq's performance on the benchmarks, see **Table 7**.

---

[3] "The Iraq Study Group Report." Vintage Books, 2006. The Iraq Study Group was funded by the conference report on P.L. 109-234, FY2006 supplemental, which provided $1 million to the U.S. Institute of Peace for operations of an Iraq Study Group. The legislation did not specify the Group's exact mandate or its composition.

The Strengthening of Maliki and Iraqi Governance: 2008-2009

The passage of Iraqi laws in 2008 considered crucial to reconciliation, continued reductions in violence accomplished by the U.S. surge, and the continued turn of many Sunni militants away from violence, enhanced Maliki's political position. A March 2008 offensive ordered by Maliki against the Sadr faction and other militants in Basra and environs ("Operation Charge of the Knights") pacified the city and caused many Sunnis and Kurds to see Maliki as even-handed— willing to take on radical groups even if they were Shiite. This contributed to a decision in July 2008 by the Sunni-led Accord Front to end its one-year boycott of the cabinet. During the period in which the Accord Front, the Sadr faction, and the bloc of former Prime Minister Iyad al-Allawi were boycotting, there were 13 vacancies out of 37 cabinet slots.

Attempts to Decentralize Governance: Provincial Powers Law and January 31, 2009, Provincial Elections

The January 31, 2009, provincial elections followed adoption in 2008 of a "provincial powers law" intended to decentralize governance by setting up powerful provincial councils that could decide local allocation of resources. The provincial councils in Iraq choose each province's governor and governing administrations—in contrast to Afghanistan, where provincial governors are appointed by the president. Some central government funds are given as grants directly to provincial administrations for their use, although most of Iraq's budget is controlled centrally. Of the provincial grants, there have been some efforts in 2012 in some provinces to consult with district and municipal level officials to assure a fair distribution of provincial resources.

The first provincial elections had originally been planned for October 1, 2008, but were delayed when Kurdish restiveness over integrating Kirkuk into the KRG caused a presidential council veto of the July 22, 2008, election law needed to hold these elections. That draft provided for equal division of power in Kirkuk (among Kurds, Arabs, and Turkomans) until its status is finally resolved, a proposal strongly opposed by the Kurds. On September 24, 2008, the COR passed a final election law, providing for the elections by January 31, 2009, and putting off provincial elections in Kirkuk and the three KRG provinces.[4]

In the elections, about 14,500 candidates vied for the 440 provincial council seats in the 14 Arab-dominated provinces of Iraq. About 4,000 of the candidates were women. The average number of council seats per province was about 30,[5] down from a set number of 41 seats per province (except Baghdad) in the 2005-2009 councils. The Baghdad provincial council has 57 seats. This yielded an average of more than 30 candidates per council seat. However, the reduction in number of seats also meant that many incumbents were not reelected.

The provincial elections were conducted on an "open list" basis—voters were able to vote for a party slate, or for an individual candidate (although they also had to vote for that candidate's slate). This procedure encouraged voting for slates and strengthened the ability of political parties to choose who on their slate will occupy seats allotted for that party. This election system was

---

[4] The election law also stripped out provisions in the vetoed version to allot 13 total reserved seats, spanning six provinces, to minorities. An October 2008 amendment restored six reserved seats for minorities: Christian seats in Baghdad, Nineveh, and Basra; one seat for Yazidis in Nineveh; one seat for Shabaks in Nineveh; and one seat for the Sabean sect in Baghdad.

[5] Each provincial council has 25 seats plus one seat per each 200,000 residents over 500,000.

widely assessed to favor larger, well-organized parties, because smaller parties might not meet the vote threshold to obtain any seats on the council in their province.[6] This was seen as likely to set back the hopes of some Iraqis that the elections would weaken the Islamist parties, both Sunni and Shiite, that have dominated post-Saddam politics.

About 17 million Iraqis (any Iraqi 18 years of age or older) were eligible for the vote, which was run by the Iraqi Higher Election Commission (IHEC). Pre-election-related violence was minimal, although five candidates were killed. There were virtually no major violent incidents on election day. Turnout was about 51%, somewhat lower than some expected. Some voters complained of being turned away at polling places because their names were not on file. Other voters had been displaced by sectarian violence and were unable to vote in their new areas of habitation.

The vote totals were finalized on February 19, 2009, and were certified on March 29, 2009. Within 15 days of that (by April 13, 2009) the provincial councils began to convene under the auspices of the incumbent provincial governor, and to elect a provincial council chairperson and deputy chairperson. Within another 30 days after that (by May 12, 2009) the provincial councils selected (by absolute majority) a provincial governor and deputy governors. The term of the provincial councils is four years from the date of their first convention.

Outcomes: Maliki Strongest Among Shiites, and Sunni Tribalists Enter Politics

The hopes of some Maliki opponents that the provincial elections would empower local authorities were dashed somewhat when Maliki's "State of Law Coalition" was the clear winner of the provincial elections. ISCI, which had already been distancing itself from its erstwhile ally, Maliki's Da'wa Party, ran under a separate slate in the provincial elections—thus splitting up the formerly powerful UIA. It fared poorly. With 28 out of the 57 total seats, the Maliki slate gained control of the Baghdad provincial council, and ran very strong in most of the Shiite provinces of the south, including Basra, where it won an outright majority (20 out of 35 seats). ISCI tied Maliki's list (seven seats each) in Najaf province, which it previously dominated and which, because of Najaf's revered status in Shiism, is considered a center of political gravity in southern Iraq. ISCI won only 3 seats on the Baghdad province council, down from the 28 it held previously, and only 5 in Basra. Some observers believe that the poor showing for ISCI was a product not only of its call for devolving power out of Baghdad, but also because of its perceived close ties to Iran, which some Iraqis believed was exercising undue influence on Iraqi politics. Others say ISCI was perceived as interested in political and economic gain for its supporters.

Although Maliki's coalition fared well, the subsequent efforts to form provincial administrations demonstrated that he still needed to strike bargains with rival factions, including Sadr, ISCI, and a Sunni list of Saleh al-Mutlaq (National Dialogue Front) that contains many ex-Baathists. The provincial administrations that took shape are discussed in **Table 5**. Aside from the victory of Maliki's slate, the unexpected strength of secular parties, such as that of former Prime Minister Iyad al-Allawi, corroborated the view that voters favored slates committed to Iraqi nationalism and strong central government.

Another important trend noted in the 2009 provincial elections was the entry of ever more Sunnis into the political process. Participating in the provincial elections were Sunni tribal leaders ("Awakening Councils") who had recruited the "Sons of Iraq" fighters and who were widely

---

[6] The threshold for winning a seat is the total number of valid votes divided by the number of seats up for election.

credited for turning Iraqi Sunnis against Al Qaeda-linked extremists in Iraq. Sunni tribalists had largely stayed out of the December 2005 elections because their attention was focused primarily on the severe violence in the Sunni provinces, particularly Anbar, and because of Al Qaeda in Iraq's admonition that Sunnis stay out of the political process. However, in the 2009 provincial elections, as the violence ebbed, tribalists offered election slates and showed strength at the expense of the established Sunni parties, particularly the Iraqi Islamic Party (IIP) and the National Dialogue Council. The main "Iraq Awakening" tribal slate came in first in Anbar Province. The tribalists benefitted from the decline of the IIP and other mostly urban Sunni parties. In Diyala Province, hotly contested among Shiite and Sunni Arab and Kurdish slates, the provincial version of the (Sunni Arab) Accord Front edged out the Kurds for first place, and subsequently allied with the Kurds and with ISCI to set up the provincial administration.

The March 7, 2010, Elections: Shiites Fracture and Sunnis Cohere

After his slate's strong showing in the January 2009 provincial elections, Maliki became the immediate favorite to retain his position in the March 7, 2010, COR elections. The elected COR chooses the full-term government. Maliki derived further political benefit from the U.S. implementation of the U.S.-Iraq "Security Agreement" (SA, sometimes referred to as the Status of Forces Agreement, or SOFA), discussed below in the section on the U.S. military mission.

However, as 2009 progressed, Maliki's image as protector of law and order was tarnished by several high-profile attacks. Realizing the potential for security lapses to reduce his chances to remain prime minister, Maliki ordered several ISF commanders questioned for lapses in connection with the major bombings in Baghdad on August 20, 2009, in which almost 100 Iraqis were killed and the buildings housing the Ministry of Finance and of Foreign Affairs were heavily damaged. Makeshift Ministry of Finance buildings were attacked again on December 7, 2009.

Politically, sensing Maliki's weakness and a more open competition for prime minister, Shiite unity broke down and a rival Shiite slate took shape as a competitor to Maliki's State of Law. The "Iraqi National Alliance (INA)" was composed of ISCI, Sadr, and other Shiite figures. The INA coalition believed that each of its component factions would draw support from their individual constituencies to produce an election majority or clear plurality.

To Sunni Arabs, the outwardly cross-sectarian Iraq National Movement ("Iraqiyya") of former transitional Prime Minister Iyad al-Allawi had strong appeal. There was an openly Sunni slate, leaning Islamist, called the Accordance slate ("Tawaffuq") led by IIP figures, but it was not expected to fare well compared to Allawi's less sectarian bloc. Some Sunni figures were recruited to join Shiite slates.

Table 1. Major Coalitions for 2010 National Elections

State of Law Coalition (slate no. 337)	Led by Maliki and his Da'wa Party. Included Anbar Salvation Front of Shaykh Hatim al-Dulaymi, which is Sunni, and the Independent Arab Movement of Abd al-Mutlaq al-Jabbouri. Appealed to Shiite sectarianism during the campaign by backing the exclusion of candidates with links to outlawed Baath Party.
Iraqi National Alliance (slate no. 316)	Formed in August 2009, was initially considered the most formidable challenger to Maliki's slate. Consisted mainly of his Shiite opponents and was perceived as somewhat more Islamist than the other slates. Included ISCI, the Sadrist movement, the Fadilah Party, the Iraqi National Congress of Ahmad Chalabi, and the National Reform Movement (Da'wa faction) of former Prime Minister Ibrahim al-Jafari. Possible potential prime ministerial candidate from this bloc was Deputy President Adel Abd al-Mahdi, a moderate well respected by U.S. officials. However, some observers say Chalabi—the key architect of the effort to exclude candidates with Baathist ties—wanted to replace Maliki. This slate was considered close to Ayatollah Sistani, but did not receive his formal endorsement.
Iraqi National Movement ("Iraqiyya"—slate no. 333)	Formed in October 2009. Led by former Prime Minister Iyad al-Allawi (Iraq National Accord) who is Shiite but his faction appeals to Sunnis, and Sunni leader Saleh al-Mutlaq (ex-Baathist who leads Iraq Front for National Dialogue). Backed by Iraqi Islamic Party leader and Deputy President Tariq Al-Hashimi as well as other powerful Sunnis, including Usama al-Nujaifi and Rafi al-Issawi. Justice and Accountability Commission (formerly the De-Baathification Commission) disqualified Mutlaq and another senior candidate on this slate, Dhafir al Ani, for supporting the outlawed Baath Party. An appeals court affirmed their disqualification, but the decision was legislatively reversed after the election).
Kurdistan Alliance (slate no. 372)	Competed again in 2010 as a joint KDP-PUK Kurdish list. However, Kurdish solidarity was shaken by July 25, 2009, Kurdistan elections in which a breakaway PUK faction called Change (Gorran) did unexpectedly well. Gorran ran its own separate list for the March 2010 elections. PUK's ebbing strength in the north did not jeopardize Talabani's continuation as president, although Sunnis sought that position.
Unity Alliance of Iraq (slate no. 348)	Led by Interior Minister Jawad Bolani, a moderate Shiite who has a reputation for political independence. Bolani was not previously affiliated with the large Shiite parties such as ISCI and Dawa, and was only briefly aligned with the Sadr faction (which has been strong in Bolani's home town of Amarah, in southeastern Iraq). Considered non-sectarian, this list included Sunni tribal faction led by Shaykh Ahmad Abu Risha, brother of slain leader of the Sunni Awakening movement in Anbar. The list included first post-Saddam defense minister Sadun al-Dulaymi.
Iraqi Accordance (slate no. 338)	A coalition of Sunni parties, including breakaway factions of the Iraqi Islamic Party (IIP). Led by Ayad al-Samarrai, then-speaker of the COR. Was viewed as a weak competitor for Sunni votes against Allawi slate.

Sources: Carnegie Endowment for International Peace; various press.

Election Law Dispute and Final Provisions

While coalitions formed to challenge Maliki, disputes emerged over the ground rules for the election. The holding of the elections required passage of an election law setting out the rules and parameters of the election. Under the Iraqi constitution, the elections were to be held by January 31, 2010, in order to allow 45 days before the March 15, 2010, expiry of the current COR's term. Iraq's election officials had ideally wanted a 90-day time frame between the election law passage and the election date, in order to facilitate the voter registration process.

Because the provisions of the election law (covering such issues as voter eligibility, whether to allot quota seats to certain constituencies, and the size of the next COR) shape the election outcome, the major Iraqi communities were divided over its substance. These differences caused the COR to miss almost every self-imposed deadline to pass it. One dispute was over the election system, with many COR members leaning toward a closed list system that gives the slates the power to determine who occupies COR seats after the election. Others, backed by Grand Ayatollah Sistani, called for an open list vote, which allows voters to also vote for candidates as well as coalition slates. Each province served as a single constituency and a fixed number of seats for each province (see **Table 2**, for the number of seats per province).

There was also a dispute over how to apply the election in disputed Tamim (Kirkuk) province, where Kurds feared that the election law drafts would cause Kurds to be underrepresented. The version of the election law passed by the COR on November 8, 2009 (141 out of 195 COR deputies voting), called for using 2009 food ration lists as representative of voter registration. The Kurds had sought this provision, facing down the insistence of many COR deputies to use 2005 voter lists, which presumably would contain fewer Kurds. A compromise in that version of the law allowed for a process to review, for one year, complaints about fraudulent registration, thus easing Sunni and Shiite Arab fears about an excessive Kurdish vote in Kirkuk.

However, this version guaranteed only a small quota of seats for Iraqis living abroad or who are displaced—and Sunnis believed they would therefore be undercounted because it was mainly Sunnis who had fled Iraq. On this basis, one of Iraq's deputy presidents, Tariq al Hashimi, a Sunni Arab, vetoed the law on November 18, 2009, sending it back to the COR. A new version was adopted on November 23, 2009, but it was viewed as even less favorable to Sunni Arabs than the first version, because it eliminated any reserved seats for Iraqis in exile. Hashimi again threatened a veto, which he was required to exercise within 10 days. As that deadline was about to lapse, the major factions, at the urging of U.S. diplomats, adopted a new law on December 6, 2009.

Election Parameters

The compromise version, not vetoed by any member of the presidency council, provided for

- Expansion of the size of the COR to 325 total seats. Of these, 310 were allocated by province, with the constituency sizes ranging from Baghdad's 68 seats to Muthanna's 7. The COR size, in the absence of a recent census, was based on taking 2005 population figures and adding 2.8% per year growth.[7]

- The remaining 15 seats were to be minority reserved seats (8) and "compensatory seats" (7)—seats allocated from "leftover" votes; votes for parties and slates that did not meet a minimum threshold to achieve any seats outright.

- No separate electoral constituency for Iraqis in exile, so Iraqis in exile had their votes counted in the provinces where these voters originated.

- An open list election system.

- An election date set for March 7, 2010.

---

[7] Analysis of Iraq expert Reidar Visser. "The Hashemi Veto." http://gulfanalysis.wordpress.com/2009/11/18/the-hashemi-veto/.

Flashpoint: De-Baathification and Disqualification of Some Prominent Sunnis

The electoral process was at least partly intended to bring Sunni Arabs ever further into the political structure and to turn them away from violence and insurgency. Sunnis boycotted the January 2005 parliamentary and provincial elections and were, as a result, poorly represented in all governing bodies. Sunni slates, consisting mainly of urban, educated Sunnis, did participate in the December 2005 parliamentary elections, an apparent calculation that it would not serve Sunni interests to remain permanently alienated from the political process.

The Sunnis' commitment to the political process appeared in some jeopardy in the context of a major dispute over candidate eligibility for the March 2010 elections. Although a Sunni boycott of the elections did not materialize, there was a Sunni Arab perception that the election might be unfair because of this dispute. The acute phase of this political crisis began in January 2010 when the Justice and Accountability Commission (JAC, the successor to the "De-Baathification Commission" that worked since the fall of Saddam to purge former Baathists from government) invalidated the candidacies of 499 individuals (out of 6,500 candidates running), spanning many different slates. The JAC was headed by Ali al-Lami, a Shiite who had been in U.S. military custody during 2005-2006 for alleged assistance to Iranian agents active in Iraq. He was perceived as answerable to or heavily influenced by Ahmad Chalabi, who had headed the De-Baathification Commission. Both were part of the Iraqi National Alliance slate and both are Shiites, leading many to believe that the disqualifications represented an attempt to exclude prominent Sunnis from the vote.

The JAC argued that the disqualifications were based on law and careful evaluation of candidate backgrounds and not based on sect, because many of the candidates disqualified were Shiites. The IHEC reviewed and backed the invalidations on January 14, 2010; disqualified candidates had three days to file an appeal in court. Apparently due in part to entreaties from Vice President Joseph Biden (during a visit to Iraq on January 22, 2010) and partner embassies in Iraq—all of which feared a return to instability—the appeals court ruled that disqualified candidates could run in the election and clear up questions of Baathist affiliation afterwards. However, about 300 disqualified candidates had already been replaced by other candidates on their respective slates. The slate most affected by the disqualifications was Iraqiyya, because two of its leading candidates, National Dialogue Front party leader Saleh al-Mutlaq and Dhafir al-Ani, both Sunnis, were replaced on their slates. Still, the slate campaigned vigorously, and many Sunnis seemed to react by recommitting to a high turnout among their community, in order to achieve political results through the election process. Even the JAC's disqualification of an additional 55 mostly Iraqiyya candidates the night before the election did not prompt a boycott.

The crisis appeared to prompt the February 16, 2010, comments by General Ray Odierno, then the top U.S. commander in Iraq (who was replaced as of September 1, 2010, by his deputy, General Lloyd Austin), that Iran was working through Chalabi and al-Lami to undermine the legitimacy of the elections. General Odierno specifically asserted that Chalabi was in close contact with an Iraqi, COR member Jamal al-Ibrahimi, who is a purported ally of General Qasem Soleimani, who commands the Qods Force unit of Iran's Islamic Revolutionary Guard Corps (IRGC).[8] Chalabi's successful efforts to turn the election into a campaign centered on excluding ex-Baathists—which Sunnis view as a codeword for their sect—caused particular U.S. alarm.

---

[8] Gertz, Bill. "Inside the Ring." *Washington Times*, February 18, 2010.

Lami was assassinated on May 26, 2011, presumably by Sunnis who viewed him as an architect of the perceived discrimination. Chalabi, a member of parliament as of the 2010 elections, initially replaced Lami as manager of the JAC, but Maliki dismissed Chalabi, appointing instead the minister for human rights to serve in that role concurrently.

Election and Results

About 85 total coalitions were accredited for the March 7, 2010, election. There were about 6,170 total candidates running on all these slates and, as noted, Iraqis were able to vote for individual candidates as well as overall slates. The major blocs are depicted in **Table 1**. All available press reports indicated that campaigning was vibrant and vigorous. Total turnout was about 62%, according to the IHEC, although somewhat lower than that in Baghdad because of the multiple insurgent bombings that took place just as voting was starting.

The final count was announced on March 26, 2010, by the IHEC. As noted in **Table 2**, Iraqiyya won a plurality of seats, winning a narrow two-seat margin over Maliki's State of Law slate. The Iraqi constitution (Article 73) mandates that the COR "bloc with the largest number" of members gets the first opportunity to form a government. On that basis, Allawi, leader of the Iraqiyya slate, demanded the first opportunity to form a government. However, on March 28, 2010, Iraq's Supreme Court issued a preliminary ruling that any group that forms after the election could be deemed to meet that requirement, laying the groundwork for Allawi to be denied the right to the first opportunity to form a government.

The vote was to have been certified by April 22, 2010, but factional disputes delayed the certification. On March 21, 2010, before the count was final, Prime Minister Maliki issued a statement, referring to his role as armed forces commander-in-chief, demanding the IHEC respond to requests from various blocs for a manual recount of all votes. The IHEC responded that a comprehensive recount would take an extended period of time. Several international observers, including then-U.N. Special Representative for Iraq Ad Melkert, indicated that there was no cause to suggest widespread fraud. (Melkert was replaced in September 2011 by Martin Kobler.)

After appeals of some of the results, Iraq's Supreme Court certified the results on June 1, 2010, triggering the following timelines:

- Fifteen days after certification (by June 15, 2010), the new COR was to be seated and to elect a COR speaker and deputy speaker. (The deadline to convene was met, although, as noted, the COR did not elect a leadership team and did not meet again until November 11, 2010.)

- After electing a speaker, but with no deadline, the COR is to choose a president (by a two-thirds vote). (According to Article 138 of the Iraqi constitution, after this election, Iraq is to have a president and at least one vice president—the "presidency council" concept was an interim measure that expired at the end of the first full-term government.)

- Within another 15 days, the largest COR bloc is tapped by the president to form a government. (The selection of a president occurred on November 11, 2010, and Maliki was formally tapped to form a cabinet on November 25, 2010.)

- Within another 30 days (by December 25, 2010), the prime minister-designate is to present a cabinet to the COR for confirmation (by majority vote).

Post-Election Government

In accordance with timelines established in the Constitution, the newly elected COR convened on June 15, 2010, but the session ended after only 18 minutes and without electing a COR leadership team. Under Article 52 of the Constitution, the "eldest member" of the COR (Kurdish legislator Fouad Massoum) became acting COR speaker. During the period when no new government was formed, the COR remained inactive, with most COR members in their home provinces while still collecting their $10,000 per month salaries. The resentment over this contributed to the popular unrest in February 2011.

Allawi's chances of successfully forming a government appeared to suffer a substantial setback in May 2010 when Maliki's slate and the rival Shiite INA bloc agreed to an alliance called the "National Alliance." However, the alliance was not able to immediately agree to a prime minister selectee. With no agreement, the COR aborted its second meeting scheduled for July 27, 2010. lliance splintered. The various factions made little progress through August 2010, as Maliki insisted he remain prime minister for another term and remained prime minister in a caretaker role. With the end of the U.S. combat mission on August 31, 2010, approaching, the United States reportedly stepped up its involvement in political talks. Some discussions were held between Maliki and Allawi's bloc on a U.S.-proposed formulas under which Allawi, in return for supporting Maliki, would head a new council that would have broad powers as a check and balance on the post of prime minister. Alternate proposals had Allawi being given the presidency, although the Kurds refused to cede that post to another community, fearing loss of leverage on other demands. An expectation that the August 10-September 11, 2010, Ramadan period would enable the blocs to reach an agreement was not met.

Part of the difficulty forming a government was the close result, and the dramatic implications of gaining or retaining power in Iraq, where politics is often seen as a "winner take all" proposition. Others blamed Allawi for the impasse, claiming that he was insisting on a large, powerful role for himself even though he could not assemble enough COR votes to achieve a majority there.

Agreement on a New Government Reached ("Irbil Agreement")

On October 1, 2010, Maliki received the backing of most of the 40 COR deputies of Shiite cleric Moqtada Al Sadr. The United States reportedly was alarmed at the prospect that Maliki might be able to form a government primarily by allying with Sadr, but it, Allawi, and the Sunni Arab regional states acquiesced to a second Maliki term. The key question that remained was whether Maliki and Iraq's Kurds would agree to form a broad based government that met the demands of Iraqiyya for substantial Sunni Arab inclusion. Illustrating the degree to which the Kurds reclaimed their former role of "kingmakers," Maliki, Allawi, and other Iraqi leaders met in the capital of the Kurdistan Regional Government-administered region in Irbil on November 8, 2010, to continue to negotiate on a new government. (Sadr did not attend the meeting in Irbil, but ISCI/Iraq National Alliance slate leader Ammar Al Hakim did.)

On November 10, 2010, with reported direct intervention by President Obama, the "Irbil Agreement" was reached in which (1) Allawi agreed to support Maliki and Talabani to remain in their offices for another term; (2) Iraqiyya would be extensively represented in government—one of its figures would become COR Speaker, another would be defense minister, and another (presumably Allawi himself) would chair the enhanced oversight body discussed above, though renamed the "National Council for Strategic Policies;"[9] and (3) amending the de-Baathification laws that had barred some Iraqis, such as Saleh al-Mutlaq, from holding political positions. Observers praised the agreement because it included all major factions and was signed with KRG President Masoud Barzani and U.S. Ambassador to Iraq James Jeffrey in attendance. The agreement did not specify concessions to the Sadr faction.

2010-2014 Government Formed[10]

At the November 11, 2010, COR session to implement the agreement, Iraqiyya figure Usama al-Nujaifi (brother of controversial Nineveh Governor Atheel Nujaifi) was elected COR speaker, as agreed. However, Allawi and most of his bloc walked out after three hours over the refusal of the other blocs to readmit the three Iraqiyya members who had been disqualified from running for the COR (see above). The remaining COR members were sufficient for a quorum and Talabani was re-elected president after two rounds of voting. Fears were further calmed on November 13, 2010, when most of Allawi's bloc attended the COR session and continued to implement the settlement agreement; Allawi himself did not attend. On November 25, 2010, Talabani formally tapped Maliki as the prime minister-designate, giving him 30 days (until December 25) to name and achieve majority COR confirmation for a new cabinet.

Governmental formation advanced on December 19, 2010, when Allawi reaffirmed his intent to join the government. His cooperation came when the COR voted (with barely a quorum achieved after a Shiite walkout) to reinstate to politics the three barred members of his bloc, discussed above. Mutlaq was subsequently named one of three deputy prime ministers.

On December 21, 2010, in advance of the December 25, 2010, deadline, Maliki presented a cabinet to the COR (42 seats, including the posts of prime minister, 3 deputy prime ministers, and 38 ministries and ministers of state) receiving broad approval. No permanent appointments were named for seven ministries. Still, the government formed was inclusive of all major factions. Among major outcomes were the following:

- As for the State of Law list, Maliki remained prime minister, and retained for himself the Defense, Interior, and National Security (minister of state) posts pending permanent nominees for those positions. The faction took seven other cabinet posts, in addition to the post of first deputy president (Khudair al Khuzai of the Da'wa Party) and deputy prime minister for energy issues (Hussein Shahristani, previously the oil minister).

- For Iraqiyya, in addition to Mutlaq becoming a deputy prime minister, Tariq al-Hashimi remained a deputy president (the second deputy). The bloc also obtained nine ministerial posts, including the key Finance Ministry (Rafi al-Issawi, previously a deputy prime minister).

---

[9] Fadel, Leila and Karen DeYoung. "Iraqi Leaders Crack Political Deadlock." *Washington Post*, November 11, 2010.

[10] The following information is taken from Iraqi news accounts presented in http://www.opensource.gov.

- For the Iraqi National Alliance, a senior figure, Adel Abdul Mahdi, remained one of the three deputy presidents. The alliance also obtained 13 cabinet positions, parceled out among its various factions. An INA technocrat, Abd al Karim Luaibi, was appointed oil minister. A Fadilah party member, Bushra Saleh, became minister of state without portfolio and the only woman in the cabinet until the February 13, 2011, naming of Ibtihal Al Zaidy as minister of state for women's affairs (not an INA member). Another Fadila activist was named minister of justice.

- Of the 13 INA cabinet seats, Sadr faction members headed eight ministries, including Housing, Labor and Social Affairs, Ministry of Planning (Ali Abd al-Nabi, appointed in April 2011), and Tourism and Antiquities. A Sadrist also is one of two deputy COR speakers. However, these positions are relatively junior within the cabinet. Still, the Sadr faction received some compensatory influence when one of its members subsequently became governor of Maysan Province.

- The Kurdistan Alliance received major posts. Talabani stayed president; and the third deputy prime minister is Kurdish figure (PUK faction) Rows Shaways, who has served in various central and KRG positions since the fall of Saddam. Arif Tayfour is second deputy COR speaker. Alliance members had six other cabinet seats, including longtime Kurdish (KDP) stalwart Hoshyar Zebari remaining as foreign minister (a position he's held since the transition governments that followed the fall of Saddam). Khairallah Hassan Babakir, was named trade minister in a February 13, 2011, group of ministerial appointments.

Unresolved Schisms and Post-U.S. Withdrawal Political Collapse

The agreements that led to the 2010 government formation did not resolve the underlying differences among the major communities. Subsequent disputes, particularly between Maliki and the Iraqiyya bloc of Iyad al-Allawi (who is Shiite but most members of the bloc are Sunnis) tarnished the U.S. assessment that Iraqi factions would permanently engage in power-sharing. The partial unraveling of the Irbil Agreement in the aftermath of the December 18, 2011, U.S. withdrawal cast some doubt on President Obama's assertion, marking the U.S. withdrawal, that Iraq is now "sovereign, stable, and self-reliant." The sections below also discuss the various disagreements and their causes.

Centralization of Power Disputes

Maliki critics cite numerous examples that demonstrate that Maliki seeks to centralize power in his own and his faction's hands. His attempts to purge leading Sunni Arabs from government are discussed below in the context of the post-U.S. withdrawal political crisis. Earlier, his critics cited his late 2010 request that Iraq's Supreme Court rule that several independent commissions—including the Independent Higher Election Commission and the anti-corruption commission—be supervised by the cabinet. The court ruled in Maliki's favor on January 23, 2011, although the court also said in its ruling that the institutions must remain free of political interference.[11] In March 2012, Maliki also asserted governmental control over another institution that was to be independent—the Central Bank.

Maliki's critics have long asserted that he has used his control over the security forces for political purposes. In 2008, he began to restructure security organs to report to his office rather than the Defense or Interior ministries. Through his Office of the Commander-in-Chief, he commands direct command of the National Counterterrorism Force (about 10,000 personnel) as well as the Baghdad Brigade, responsible for security in the capital. Reports quoting U.S. commanders in Iraq in June 2011 said that lower-level commanders routinely bypass the official chain of command and report directly to Maliki's office. On at least one occasion, he has sometimes ordered tanks deployed around the homes and offices of an opponent.

The manifestations of this basic dispute over Maliki's authority has taken several forms:

- *Security Ministerial Appointments*. Maliki's critics accuse him of monopolizing control of the major security posts. Maliki refutes Allawi's interpretation of the Irbil Agreement as requiring appointment of an Iraqiyya official as defense minister, asserting that a Sunni Arab, not necessarily a member of the Iraqiyya faction, is required. With this dispute unresolved, Maliki has appointed allies and associates as acting ministers of Defense, of Interior, and of National Security. On August 16, 2011, Maliki appointed Sadun Dulaymi as acting defense minister—he is a Sunni Arab but he is a member of the Iraq Unity Alliance, not Iraqiyya. Maliki subsequently appointed Falih al-Fayad, a Shiite in the faction of former Prime Minister Ibrahim al-Jafari, as acting minister of state for national security, and Adnan al-Asadi, another Shiite aligned with Maliki, as acting interior minister. No permanent choices for any of these posts have been nominated to date.

- *National Council for Strategic Policies*. Another issue has been the stalemate over the formation of the National Council for Strategic Policies—a key provision of the Irbil Agreement. Some proposals from those sympathetic to Allawi called for the council to include the prime minister, president, their deputies, and a representative of all major blocs—and for decisions of the council to be binding on Maliki if they achieve support of 80% of the council members. Maliki and his supporters want this council to have as few powers as possible so as not to impinge upon the power of the prime minister. The body and its powers have not been voted on by the COR, and Allawi was always considered unlikely to chair the body unless it is given significant authorities. There has been no movement on this issue at all in 2012.

- *Sunni Moves to Form Separate Regions*. In late 2011, local Sunni leaders attempted to use legal mechanisms to reduce central government control. The provincial council of the mostly Sunni province of Salahuddin (which contains Tikrit) voted on October 28, 2011, to start the process of forming a separate "region." Overwhelmingly Sunni Anbar province followed suit. The mixed province of Diyala took a similar step on December 12, 2011, setting off protests by Shiites in the province who might have been instigated by the Shiite-

---

[11] Parker, Ned and Salar Jaff. "Electoral Ruling Riles Maliki's Rivals." *Los Angeles Times*, January 23, 2011.

dominated central government. Sunni members of the provincial council subsequently fled into the Kurdish controlled areas just north of Diyala. Previously, the mostly Shiite provinces of Basra and Wasit had begun similar processes, although doing so requires parliamentary concurrence and a popular referendum of approval. The Maliki government has essentially ignored these votes and has not tasked the Independent Higher Election Commission (IHEC), which is a central government body, to organize the referenda needed as part of the region formation process. The IHEC is subject to Maliki's control, giving him a de-facto veto over the region formation process.

Post-U.S. Withdrawal Political Crisis

The political disputes discussed above intensified as U.S. forces drew down until the final withdrawal on December 18, 2011. As the last U.S. forces were exiting, and even as Maliki visited Washington, DC, on December 12, 2011, to meet with President Obama, the carefully constructed political power-sharing arrangements were breaking down. As a part of what Sunni Iraqis—and also KRG President Barzani—have called a clear power grab by Maliki, Iraq is in the midst of its worst political crisis since the U.S. invasion of 2003, and it is still possible that the Iraqi central government might unwind completely. Still, Iraqi factions have, in the past, cobbled together agreements when faced with the alternative of political collapse.

The day of the final U.S. withdrawal (December 18, 2011), Maliki asked the COR to vote no confidence against Deputy Prime Minister Saleh al-Mutlaq, a senior Iraqiyya figure and prominent Sunni (discussed above in the 2010 election disqualification crisis). That day, Iraqiyya parliamentarians walked out of the COR and most of the Iraqiyya members of the cabinet suspended their work. On December 19, 2011, the government announced an arrest warrant against Deputy President Tariq al-Hashimi, another major Iraqiyya figure, accusing him of ordering his security staff to commit acts of assassination. Three such guards were shown on television "confessing" to assassinating rival politicians at Hashimi's behest. Hashimi fled to the KRG region for meetings with President Talabani and refused to return to face trial in Baghdad, as is demanded by the judiciary, unless his conditions for a fair trial there are met. On several occasions, Maliki threatened the Kurds with unspecified action if they continue to shelter Hashimi. One theme he stressed in a December 21, 2011, news conference, which was praised by U.S. officials, was that he envisions a government in which each faction works on behalf of the country and not its own interests. The assertion that Maliki sought a comprehensive purge of Sunnis gained additional strength during January 19-20, 2012, when security forces raided the homes of two Sunni politicians in Diyala province and arrested the Sunni vice chairman of the Baghdad provincial council.

With political inclusiveness seeming to unravel, U.S. officials, including Vice President Biden, attempted to promote a peaceful resolution to the crisis. The Vice President's efforts were joined by Ambassador James F. Jeffrey, and CIA Director Petraeus, who traveled to Iraq in late December 2011 for meetings with some of the close contacts Petraeus he developed when he was overall U.S. commander in Iraq. On January 5, 2012, Ambassador Jeffrey tried to calm tensions by stating that the Maliki government appears to be allowing the judiciary to conduct a fair investigation of the charges against Hashimi—an indication that the United States does not necessarily concur with the Sunni view that the arrest warrant represented a power grab by Maliki. Deputy President Hashimi remained in KRG-controlled territory until early April 2012, when he left for Qatar, Saudi Arabia, and then Turkey, where he remains. Some criticized the

Administration for failing to rein in Maliki's efforts against his opponents by muting its opposition to his moves against them.

The Crisis Abates but Defies Resolution

The U.S. diplomatic intervention—as well as the fear among all Iraqi factions of sparking all-out political warfare—seemed to calm the crisis somewhat, although only temporarily. Iraqiyya COR deputies resumed their duties in late January 2012. The Iraqiyya ministers returned to their offices on February 8, 2012. For his part, Maliki arranged the release of some of the Baathists arrested in early 2012 and he agreed to legal amendments to give provinces more autonomy over their budgets and the right of consent when national security forces are deployed.[12]

In a potentially positive sign for Iraqi democracy amid the crisis, a cross-sectarian, secular political opposition party called the Union of Patriotic Figures was formed on February 12, 2012. It announced that it would monitor both the government and the COR.

By March 2012, the easing of the crisis appeared to pave the way for the start of a "national conference" to be chaired by President Talabani, the purpose of which would be to achieve durable solutions to the outstanding fundamental Sunni-Shiite-Kurdish issues. A "preparatory committee" was named to establish an agenda and format, but the committee repeatedly failed to meet. The March 20, 2012, comments by KRG President Barzani, accusing Maliki of a power grab by harnessing control of the security forces, dimmed prospects for holding the conference were dim. On April 1, 2012, Maliki nonetheless formally issued invitations to the major factions to convene on April 5, 2012. Barzani kept intact his plans to visit the United States at that time and the conference was not held, nor was a new date for it set.

During April 27-28, Maliki critics met in the KRG region at the invitation of Barzani. Also attending the meetings were Iraqiyya leader Allawi, Iraqiyya member and COR speaker Nujaifi, and Moqtada Al Sadr, in what reportedly was his first ever visit to the Kurdish north. At the conclusion of the meetings, the four reportedly issued a letter to Maliki threatening a vote of no-confidence within 15 days unless he adheres to the "principles and framework" of a more democratic approach to governance.

During late May and early June 2012, the Maliki opponents obtained the signature of 176 deputies requesting a no-confidence vote. Under Article 61 of the constitution, signatures of only 20% of the 325 COR deputies (65 signatures) are needed to trigger a vote, but President Talabani, who is required to present a valid request to the COR to hold the vote, determined that factions must demonstrate they have enough support to win such a vote. On June 10, 2012, Talabani stated that there were only 160 valid signatures, after some deputies asked their signatures be removed. On that basis he declined to ask the COR to go forward with the no-confidence vote. Some experts attributed the signature withdrawals to pressure by Iran, through the Sadr faction, to keep Maliki in office.[13] Some Maliki opponents may have been dissuaded from continuing the effort by Maliki's counter-threat to call early national elections. This suggested that Maliki believed the political battle has solidified his popularity with much of the Shiite community. On the other hand, one rival Shiite leaders, ISCI's leader Ammar al-Hakim, proved an able and successful mediator, perhaps in an effort to position himself for national leadership in the future elections.

---

[12] Tim Arango. "Iraq's Prime Minister Gains More Power After Political Crisis." *New York Times*, February 28, 2012.

[13] "Embattled Iraqi PM Holding On To Power for Now." Associated Press, June 12, 2012.

In part to cause the no-confidence vote effort to falter, or to calm the political situation in general, some observers say Maliki has reached out to Sunni leaders. The Hashimi trial in absentia began in Baghdad in early May 2012 and Maliki reportedly has succeeded in convincing observers that there is evidence to support the allegations against Hashimi. The Iraqi court trying him sentenced Hashimi to death on September 9, 2012 for the killing of two Iraqis. Deputy Prime Minister Saleh al-Mutlaq has resumed his duties, signaling an end to another of Maliki's efforts against Sunni leadership figures. And, Iraqi news sources said that Maliki was able to win the support of two other senior Iraqiyya figures in early September 2012—COR Speaker Osama al-Nujaifi and Finance Minister Rafi al-Issawi. On the other hand, Minister of Communications Mohammad al-Allawi, an Iraqiyya member, resigned in late August 2012 in protest of what he said was Maliki's interference in the work of his ministry.

Effect of the Crisis on Upcoming Elections

The political crisis could have a direct effect on several upcoming elections in Iraq. The mandate of the current nine-member IHEC expired at the end of April 2012. The April 12, 2012 arrest of the IHEC chairman, Faraj al-Haidari, threatened to complicate the naming of a new panel, but he was released and had resumed his duties by April 15, 2012. In late April, the IHEC's mandate was extended by three months, and the COR confirmed a new panel in September 2012. The IHEC is needed to run the upcoming elections scheduled or possible.

KRG Elections. Provincial elections in the KRG-controlled provinces were not held during the January 2009 provincial elections in the other areas of Iraq, nor were they held during the March 7, 2010, COR vote. These elections were scheduled for September 27, 2012 but a June 2012 announcement postponement them indefinitely. Kurdish officials postponed them because the IHEC had ruled that Christian voters could only vote for Christian candidates, a ruling the Kurds said restricted the rights of minorities living in the KRG.

Provincial Elections. As noted above, the terms of the provincial councils are four years. New provincial elections in the central government controlled provinces are due by early 2013.

Kirkuk Referendum. There is also to be a vote on a Kirkuk referendum at some point, if a negotiated settlement is reached. However, a settlement does not appear within easy reach as of early 2012 and no referendum is scheduled.

District and Sub-District Elections. District and sub-district elections throughout Iraq were previously slated for July 31, 2009. However, those have been delayed as well, and no date has been announced.

Constitutional Amendments. There could also be a vote on amendments to Iraq's 2005 constitution if and when the major factions agree to finalize the recommendations of the constitutional review commission (CRC). There has been no movement on this issue for at least three years, and no indication such a referendum will be held in the near future.

Next National Elections. The term of the existing COR expires no later than early 2014, but, depending on when applicable election laws are adopted, and subject to negotiations among the factions, the next COR elections might be held in late 2013. That schedule could change if the political crisis leads to early elections, as discussed above.

Broader Sunni Community Grievances and Escalating Violence

Aside from the disputes between Sunni elites and Maliki, there is a broad sense among many Iraqi Sunnis that Maliki and his Shiite allies want to monopolize power. As the U.S. withdrawal completion approached, fears of some Sunnis were inflamed in October and November 2011 by a series of arrests by security forces. About 600 Sunnis were arrested, ostensibly for involvement in a coup plot alleged by the new leaders of Libya. Some Sunnis were reportedly purged from the security forces, and 140 faculty members from the University of Tikrit (Saddam's home town) were removed for alleged Baathist associations. Many of the latter have since been reinstated. These sentiments continue to plague post-U.S. presence Iraq.

Sunni Insurgent Violence/Al Qaeda in Iraq (AQ-I) and Naqshabandis

The suspicions of the Sunni community might account for some of the high-profile attacks that continue in Iraq, including those carried out by Al Qaeda in Iraq (AQ-I). U.S. officials estimated in November 2011 that there might be 800-1,000 people in Al Qaeda-Iraq's network, of which many are involved in media or finance of operations.[14]

Another Sunni group, linked to ex-Baathists, is the Naqshabandi faction, based in northern Iraq. Former Ambassador-nominee to Iraq Brett McGurk said in his June 6, 2012, confirmation hearings that the Naqshabandis are responsible for most of the attacks on U.S. diplomatic facilities in northern Iraq (particularly Kirkuk), although such attacks number only about 2-3 per week, a relatively low level compared to periods at the height of the U.S. military mission in Iraq. The attacks might have contributed to the State Dept. decision in 2012 to close the Kirkuk consulate.

Since the completion of the U.S. withdrawal on December 18, 2011, these Sunni groups, particularly AQ-I, have been conducting numerous high-profile suicide and other attacks against Shiite religious pilgrims and neighborhoods throughout Iraq. These attacks are perceived as an effort by Sunni insurgents and AQ-I to undermine Maliki's leadership; to retaliate against his perceived actions against Sunnis; to dissuade moderate Sunnis from continuing to work with Maliki's government; and to possibly reignite sectarian conflict. The attacks have not, to any significant extent, accomplished those objectives to date.

Some assert that AQ-I and other Sunni insurgent groups have been emboldened by the civil conflict in Syria, in which Sunni insurgents are challenging the Assad regime, which is linked to Shiite Iran. In sympathy with the Sunni-led "Free Syrian Army" armed opposition in Syria, some Iraqi groups have begun referring to themselves as the "Free Iraqi Army."

Significant Increase in Violence in 2012

As the conflict in Syria and the political disputes in Iraq have continued, large scale attacks have been increasing in Iraq. On February 7, 2012, the AQ-I affiliate Islamic State of Iraq claimed responsibility for two of the deadliest attacks on Shiites since the U.S. withdrawal—January 5 and January 14, 2012 attacks that killed 78 and 53 Shiite pilgrims, respectively. In one of the most

---

[14] Michael Schmidt and Eric Schmitt. "Leaving Iraq, U.S. Fears New Surge of Qaeda Terror." *New York Times*, November 6, 2011.

complex attacks in recent months, on February 23, 2012, bombings attributed to AQ-I in 12 Iraqi cities killed over 50 people. AQ-I claimed responsibility for a broad series of attacks—encompassing six cities—on March 20, 2012; over 40 people were killed. Another spate of attacks took place in Baghdad and Kirkuk on April 19, 2012, killing about 36 people. On June 12, 2012, in attacks that bear the hallmarks of AQ-I, there were separate bombings in numerous cities, targeting Shiite pilgrims, killing about 65 and wounding 200. This attack came about one week after a bombing of a Shiite religious office that sought to take control of administering the Shiite mosque in Salahuddin that was bombed in 2006 (see above). On July 4, 2012, attacks throughout Iraq killed about 50 people, primarily Shiites killed in the bombs set off in Diwaniya.

The summer of 2012 saw numerous major attacks. One was on July 23, 2012, in which AQ-I conducted numerous attacks in several cities, killing about 115 Iraqis; the attacks came a day after AQ-I leader Abu Bakr Al Baghdadi announced a "Breaking Down Walls" offensive against government targets. Shortly thereafter, Iraqi insurgents downed an Iraqi helicopter. In late July 2012, the AQ-I offensive compelled 15 Diyala Province *"mukhtars"*- chosen community liaisons with the central government—to resign, claiming the government is not able to protect them. In mid-August, AQ-I insurgents briefly captured a local government building in Haditha (Anbar Province) and raised an Al Qaeda battle flag over it. On August 17, 2012, 93 Iraqis, mostly in Shiite areas, were killed in a wide range of attacks around Iraq. On September 9, 2012, bombings in numerous cities, and attributed to AQ-I, again killed more than 100 Iraqis. Another 26 Iraqis were killed on September 30, 2012, a few days after insurgents attacked a jail in the Sunni-inhabited town of Tikrit (Saddam Hussein's home town) and freed 47 suspected AQ-I militants. Observers say that more Iraqis (more than 200) were killed in militant attacks in September 2012 than any time in the past two years.

Prior to the spate of major attacks in summer of 2012, U.S. officials asserted that, by U.S. measures of "security incidents" (attacks against diplomats, the government, or civilians) levels of violence had not increased since the U.S. pullout, and remained roughly at a post-2003 low of about 100 such incidents per week. However, the intensity of the summer 2012 attacks have produced a reassessment of that analysis. A visit to Iraq by Chairman of the Joint Chiefs of Staff Martin Dempsey on August 21, 2012, appeared intended to respond to Iraqi overtures to re-engage of some of the U.S. military and police training programs that have languished throughout 2012—overtures motivated by increasing Iraqi nervousness about the ability of the Iraq Security Forces (ISF) to prevent further such incidents.

Still, many Iraqi Sunnis do not want the AQ-I campaigns to succeed and are inclined to work with the government against AQ-I. In early 2012, more than 60 leaders of tribes in Sunni-dominated areas of Iraq—with the concurrence of local government and security officials—reached agreement to authorize tribal leaders to enforce strict codes of justice against insurgents and their accomplices. Suggesting that the attacks may be intended to dissuade moderate Sunnis from engaging with the government, one such moderate Sunni cleric, Shaykh Mahdi al-Sumaidaie, was seriously injured in a bomb attack against his convoy on August 19, 2012.

Since early 2012, there have been indications that AQ-I might be intervening in the unrest in Syria.[15] Director of National Intelligence James Clapper testified on February 16, 2012, that it might have been responsible for several suicide bombings against security targets in Damascus.

---

[15] Sahar Issa. "Iraq Violence Dips Amid Rise in Syria." Philadelphia Inquirer, February 21, 2012.

Iraq's position on the Syria unrest is discussed in greater detail below. In July 2012, Iraqi Foreign Minister Hoshyar Zebari corroborated the U.S. accusations about AQ-I movement into Syria.

Sons of Iraq Fighters

One of the most significant long-standing Sunni grievances has been the slow pace with which the Maliki government implemented its pledge to fully integrate the approximately 100,000 "Sons of Iraq" fighters (former insurgents who ended their fight and cooperated with U.S. forces against Al Qaeda in Iraq and other militants) into the Iraqi Security Forces (ISF) or provide them with government jobs. During 2009 and 2010, there were repeated reports that some Sons of Iraq had been dropped from payrolls, harassed, arrested, or sidelined, and that the Maliki government might want to strangle the program. However, according to Ambassador-nominee Brett McGurk in confirmation hearings on June 6, 2012, about 70,000 have been integrated into the ISF or given civilian government jobs, while 30,000 continue to man checkpoints in Sunni areas and are paid about $300 per month by the government.

KRG-Central Government Disputes[16]

The United States has played a role since 1991 of protecting Iraq's Kurds from the central government. Iraq's Kurds have tried to preserve this "special relationship" with the United States and use it to their advantage. Iraq's Kurdish leaders have long said they do not seek outright independence or affiliation with Kurds in neighboring countries, but the Iraqi Kurds seek to preserve and expand on the autonomy they have achieved since 1991. The issues dividing the KRG and Baghdad include not only KRG autonomy but also disputes over territory and resources, including the ability of the KRG to export its oil. That difference underpins KRG-Baghdad disagreements over proposed national oil laws.

The increasing disillusionment of Kurdish leaders with Maliki could produce major political unraveling. During 2012, the Kurds have adopted the Sunni Arab criticisms of Maliki. KRG President Masoud Barzani, who was directly elected by the residents of the Kurdish region in July 2009, hinted at a potential break with Maliki on March 20, 2012, accusing him of monopolizing power. Following a visit to Washington, DC, in early April 2012, Barzani indirectly threatened to allow a vote on Kurdish independence unless Maliki resolves these issues with the KRG before the Kurdish provincial elections in September 2012. [17] In June 2012, the Kurds in the COR joined Iraqiyya in a move, thus far unsuccessful, to vote no confidence against Maliki. There had been a historic hesitancy among the Kurds to side with the Sunni Arabs because of the legacy of repression of the Kurds by Saddam Hussein and other Sunni Iraqi leaders in the past.

Very few experts predict that these differences will produce all-out violent conflict between the KRG and Baghdad. However, in part to deter that possibility, the two main Kurdish factions (Patriotic Union of Kurdistan, PUK, and Kurdistan Democratic Party, KDP) continue to field their own force of *peshmerga* (Kurdish militiamen) numbering perhaps 75,000 fighters. They are generally lightly armed.

---

[16] For more information on Kurd-Baghdad disputes, see CRS Report RS22079, *The Kurds in Post-Saddam Iraq*, by Kenneth Katzman.

[17] Interview with Masoud Barzani by Hayder al-Khoie on Al-Hurra television network. April 6, 2012.

At the same time, the Iraqi Kurds are increasingly being drawn into the conflict in Syria. Thousands of Syrian Kurds have been given refuge in the KRG. KRG President Barzani, whose KDP is prominent in the areas bordering Syria, has provided training for Syrian Kurdish guerrillas who are preparing to administer Kurdish territory in a post-Assad Syria.

Territorial Issues/"Disputed Internal Boundaries"

There has been virtually no progress in recent years in resolving the various territorial disputes between the Kurds and Iraq's Arabs—the most emotional of which is the Kurdish insistence that Tamim Province (which includes oil-rich Kirkuk) be formally affiliated to the KRG. There was to be a census and referendum on the affiliation of the province by December 31, 2007, in accordance with Article 140 of the Constitution, but the Kurds have agreed to repeated delays in order to avoid jeopardizing overall progress in Iraq. Nor has the national census that is pivotal to any such referendum been conducted. It was scheduled to begin on October 24, 2010, but was then postponed until at least December 2010 to allow time for a full-term government to be put in place. It still has not begun, in part because of the broader political crisis (discussed below) as well as differences over how to account for movements of populations into or out of the Kurdish controlled provinces.

In the absence of movement on a process to integrate Kirkuk, the Kurds have attempted to steadily assert control in the province. The current governor of Kirkuk is Najmaddin Karim, a longtime Kurdish activist in the United States before he moved back to Iraq following the fall of Saddam Hussein. The Property Claims Commission that is adjudicating claims from the Saddam regime's forced resettlement of Arabs into the KRG region is functioning. Of the 178,000 claims received, nearly 26,000 were approved and 90,000 rejected or ruled invalid, as of the end of 2011, according to the State Department human rights report for 2011. Since 2003, more than 28,000 Iraqi Arabs settled in the KRG area by Saddam have relocated from Kirkuk back to their original provinces. Attempting to resolve these long-standing disputes is another issue within the mandate of UNAMI, and consultations with all parties are ongoing, according to UNAMI.[18]

Combined Security Mechanism at Kurd-Arab Frontier

In the absence of resolution, the territorial disputes have grown more acute since the 2009 provincial elections, in which Sunni Arabs wrested back control of the Nineveh (Mosul) provincial council from the Kurds. The Kurds had won control of that council in the 2005 election because of the broad Sunni Arab boycott of that election. A Sunni list (al-Hadba'a) won a clear plurality of the 2009 Nineveh vote and subsequently took control of the provincial administration there. Al-Hadba'a is composed of hardline Sunni Arabs who openly oppose Kurdish encroachment in the province and who are committed to the "Arab and Islamic identity" of the province. A member of the faction, Atheel al-Nufaiji, is the governor (brother of 2010-2014 COR speaker Usama al-Nujaifi), and the Kurds have been preventing his visitation of areas of Nineveh where the Kurds' *peshmerga* militia operates. In October 2011, the central government ordered the Kurdish flags taken down from public buildings in Khanaqin, a Kurdish town in the province; the Kurdish police in the city disobeyed the order.

---

[18] Meeting with congressional staff, February 24, 2011.

In part to prevent outright violence between the KRG and the central government, in August 2009 then-top U.S. commander in Iraq General Raymond Odierno developed a plan to partner U.S. forces with *peshmerga* units and with ISF units in the province to build confidence along the frontier between the two forces. The process was also intended to reassure Kurdish, Arab, Turkomen, and other province residents. Implementation of this "combined security mechanism" (CSM) began in January 2010, consisting of joint (ISF-U.S-Kurdish) patrols, maintenance of 22 checkpoints, and U.S. training of participating ISF and *peshmerga* forces. The mechanism has been administered through provincial level Combined Coordination Centers. Disagreements are referred to a Senior Working Group and a High Level Ministerial Committee.[19] As of October 2010, the United States had ceased participating at four of the checkpoints, in concert with the U.S. change of mission to a non-combat role (Operation New Dawn) on September 1, 2010.

Many who asserted that at least some U.S. forces should remain in Iraq after 2011 did so on the grounds that U.S. troops are needed to continue to participate in CSM operations.[20] However, Major General David Perkins, commander of the 5,000 U.S. forces then in northern Iraq, said on September 29, 2011, that the CSM continued to work well even after U.S. forces ceased participating in the remaining joint checkpoints and patrols, and that there is not the need for a substantial U.S. force in northern Iraq after 2011. The headquarters of the 750 U.S. troops in the north closed on October 20, 2011.

The United States continues to participate in the process despite the completion of the U.S. withdrawal from Iraq in December 2011. Through Office of Security Cooperation—Iraq (OSC-I) facilities in Nineveh Province, the United States helps coordinate the joint patrols and checkpoints even though no U.S. forces participate in them. Previously, some have advanced alternatives to U.S. force participation in the CSM, including giving the U.S. role to a United Nations force, NATO, or civilians (Iraqi or international). It is not clear that any of these alternative ideas are supported by Iraqi factions.

Kurdish leaders continue to criticize Maliki for opposing paying the *peshmerga* out of the national budget, leaving the KRG to fund its operations. KRG President Barzani, during his U.S. visit in April 2012, discussed the reform of the *peshmerga* into a smaller but more professional and well trained force.

KRG Oil Exports/Oil Laws

The KRG and Baghdad have had repeated disputes over the ability of the Kurds to export oil that is discovered and extracted in the KRG region. The Kurds view it as their right to develop their resources, whereas Baghdad fears Kurdish oil exports can potentially enable the Kurds to set up an economically-viable independent state. Under a longstanding Baghdad-KRG agreement, revenues from KRG oil exports go into central government accounts, which distributes proceeds to the KRG and pays the international oil companies working in the KRG.

Oil exports from the KRG have been repeatedly suspended, for varying periods of time, over central government withholding of payments to the international energy firms. The latest such suspension of oil exports through the national oil grid began in April 2012 after the KRG accused Baghdad of falling $1.5 billion in arrears to the companies extracting oil in the KRG region. At

---

[19] "Managing Arab-Kurd Tensions in Northern Iraq After the Withdrawal of U.S. Troops." Rand Corporation, 2011.
[20] Ibid.

the time of the suspension, KRG oil exports had reached about 175,000 barrels of crude oil per day. The dispute escalated in July 2012 when the KRG began exporting crude oil by road to Turkey, some of which is being refined and returned as gasoline to the KRG region. At the same time, the Kurds are reportedly building their own oil pipeline to the Turkish border that would reduce their dependence on the national oil export grid.[21] The dispute was defused temporarily in August 2012, Kurdish exports through the national grid resumed on August 9, 2012 amid a KRG threat to conduct another halt by September 15 if the international companies were not paid. A Baghdad-KRG agreement of September 14, 2012 headed off another shutdown—the pact provided for the Kurds to raise exports to 200,000 barrels per day as of October 1, 2012, to increase that to 250,000 barrels per day for 2013, and for Baghdad to pay about $900 million in arrears due the international firms. Some experts say the KRG has potential to increase exports to 500,000 barrels per day by the end of 2013, and 1 million barrels per day by 2019.[22]

The September 2012 KRG-Baghdad agreement also instilled new hope for resolving their differences over national oil laws. The KRG adopted its own oil laws in 2007. The Kurds oppose oil laws adopted by the Iraqi cabinet in late August 2011, and sent on to the COR for ratification, as favoring a centralized energy sector that would impinge on KRG control of its energy resources. In connection with the visit of KRG Prime Minister Barham Salih, Kurdish representatives said on November 8, 2011, that it is likely that the oil laws would be taken up by the COR by the end of 2011.[23] In part due to the political crisis, the issue did not progress. However, the Baghdad-KRG agreement in September 2012 included a provision to set up a six member committee to review the different versions of the oil laws under consideration and decide which version to submit to the COR for formal consideration.

Other aspect of the dispute do not appear close to resolution. The October 2011 KRG signing of an energy development deal with U.S. energy giant Exxon-Mobil represents a further dimension of the energy row with Baghdad. The central government denounced the deal as illegal, in part because the oil fields involved are in or very close to disputed territories. The KRG has sought to defuse this consideration by saying that if the territory of the oil fields is subsequently judged to be part of central government-administered territory, then the revenues would be reallocated accordingly. Still, the central government threatened to cancel the firm's existing contract to develop the West Qurna oil field near Basra, which was signed with the central government. On February 13, 2012, the central government announced its sanction against the firm as a prohibition on bidding for work on unexplored fields to be tendered later in 2012. On March 17, 2012, Baghdad claimed that Exxon-Mobil had frozen the KRG contract, but the KRG denies the company has stopped work in the KRG region. Further disputes occurred over a July 2012 KRG deal with Total SA of France; in August 2012 the central government told Total SA to either terminate its arrangement with the KRG or give up work on the central government Halfaya field.

Intra-Kurdish Divisions

Further complicating the political landscape are widening divisions within the Kurdish community. The KRG elections also, to some extent, shuffled the political landscape. A breakaway faction of President Talabani's PUK, called "Change" ("Gorran"), won an

---

[21] International Crisis Group. "Iraq and the Kurds: The High-Stakes Hydrocarbons Gambit." April 19, 2012.

[22] Jane Arraf. "Iraq's Unity Tested by Rising Tensions Over Oil-Rich Kurdish Region." *Christian Science Monitor,* May 4, 2012.

[23] Author conversation with KRG Washington, DC, representative Qubad Talabani, November 8, 2011.

unexpectedly high 25 seats (out of 111) in the Kurdistan national assembly, embarrassing the PUK and weakening it relative to the KDP. KRG President Masoud Barzani, leader of the KDP, easily won reelection against weak opposition. Gorran ran its own list in the March 2010 elections and constituted a significant challenge to the Kurdistan Alliance in Sulaymaniyah Province, according to election results. As a result, of the 57 COR seats held by Kurds, 14 are held by parties other than the Kurdistan Alliance. Gorran has 8, the Kurdistan Islamic Union has 4, and the Islamic Group of Kurdistan has 2.

These divisions may also have played a role in the popular demonstrations that occurred in Sulaymaniyah in early 2011. The demonstrations reflected frustration over jobs and services but possibly also over the monopolization of power in the KRG by the Barzani and Talabani clans. Some of these were suppressed by *peshmerga.*

The Sadr Faction's Continuing Ambition and Agitation

Within the broader Shiite community, the faction of Shiite cleric, Moqtada Al Sadr, who is about 37 years old, sees itself as the main representative for Iraq's Shiites, particularly those who are poor or working class. This has caused an inherent rivalry with Maliki and other Shiite leaders in Iraq. Although Sadr was part of the anti-Maliki Shiite coalition (Iraqi National Alliance) for the March 2010 national elections, he reached a political arrangement with Maliki that paved the way for Maliki's achieving another term. Sadrists were given several seats in the cabinet and a Sadrist governor was later installed in Maysan Province, which includes the Sadrist stronghold of Amarah.

Suggesting that Sadr often shifts so as to maximize his faction's leverage, in May 2012 Sadr himself participated in meetings in the KRG region with other anti-Maliki factions to put pressure on Maliki to increase power sharing. In June 2012, Sadrist deputies in the COR signed onto a letter requesting a vote of no-confidence against Maliki, discussed further below. However, Iranian figures, including Sadr's mentor, Ayatollah Abdol Kazem Haeri, successfully persuaded Sadr to end his discussions with Maliki's opponents and rally behind him. However, many experts believe Sadr could still shift against Maliki again if doing so benefits his faction.

Sadr's political shift against Maliki represents a continuation of a high level of activity he has exhibited since he returned to Iraq, from his studies in Iran, in January 2011. After his return, he gave numerous speeches that, among other themes, insisted on full implementation of a planned U.S. withdrawal by the end of 2011. Sadr's position on the U.S. withdrawal appeared so firm that, in an April 9, 2011, statement, he threatened to reactivate his Mahdi Army militia if U.S. forces remained in Iraq beyond the December 31, 2011, deadline. His followers conducted a large march in Baghdad on May 26, 2011, demanding a full U.S. military exit. The threats were pivotal to the Iraqi decision not to retain U.S. troops in Iraq beyond 2011.

Sadr's threats to instigate violence were considered not idle. In June and July 2011, U.S. officials accused Shiite militia offshoots of Sadr's Mahdi Army militia of causing an elevated level of U.S. troop deaths in June 2011 (14 killed, the highest in any month in over one year). These militias operate under names including Asa'ib Ahl al-Haq (AAH, League of the Righteous), Khata'ib Hezbollah (Hezbollah Battalions), and Promised Day Brigade. U.S. officials accused Iran of arming the militias with upgraded rocket-propelled munitions, such as Improvised Rocket Assisted Munitions (IRAMs), in an effort to ensure a full U.S. withdrawal and to claim credit for forcing that withdrawal. U.S. officials reportedly requested that the ISF act against these militias and to prevail on Iran to stop aiding the militias, actions that subsequently, but temporarily, quieted the Shiite attacks on U.S. forces in Iraq. Some rocket attacks continued against the U.S. consulate in Basra, which has nearly 1,000 U.S. personnel (including contractors). However, Ambassador-nominee McGurk stated at his confirmation hearings on June 6, 2012, that AAH, Khata'ib Hezbollah, and Promised Day Brigade had all become less active since the U.S. military withdrawal because the U.S. exit removed their justification for armed activity. Sadr's Mahdi Army has integrated into the political process in the form of a charity and employment network called *Mumahidoon* or "those who pave the way."

Related Governance Issues

The political crisis has dashed hopes that Iraq was well on its way to permanent stability, to strengthening democracy and institution-building, and to enabling Iraqi official attention to toward basic governance and economic issues. That hope was expressed by President Obama after his meeting with Prime Minister Maliki on December 12, 2011, and in President Obama's statement marking the December 18, 2011, completion of the withdrawal that Iraq is "sovereign, stable, and self-reliant."

National Oil Laws and Other Pending Laws

Adopting national oil laws has been considered key to attracting foreign investment in Iraq's sizeable energy resources. Substantial progress appeared near in August 2011 when both the COR and the cabinet drafted the oil laws long in the works to rationalize the energy sector and clarify the rules for foreign investors. However, there were differences in their individual versions: the version drafted by the Oil and Natural Resources Committee was presented to the full COR on August 17, 2011. The cabinet adopted its separate version on August 28, 2011; there was some expectation that the COR would take up the issue when it reconvened on September 6, 2011, after the Eid al-Fitr celebration marking the end of Ramadan. It was unclear which version would form the basis of final legislation, amid opposition from the Kurds to what they see as an overly centralized energy industry encapsulated in the cabinet's draft law. The opposition and the presence of two competing versions of the oil laws accounted for the postponement of further COR action until at least the end of 2011, and the political crisis prevented movement on it subsequently. However, as discussed in the section on the KRG and its oil exports, as of mid-September 2012, a six member panel has been empowered to review the competing versions and decide which version the COR will consider.

Also not passed are laws addressing the environment, other elections, consumer protections, intellectual property rights, building codes, and the permanent rules for de-Baathification. Others say that the failure to adopt new laws governing investment, taxation, and property ownership account for the slow pace of building a modern, dynamic economy, although others say the success of Iraq's energy sector is overriding these adverse factors. On the other hand, on April 30, 2012, the COR enacted a law to facilitate elimination of trafficking in persons, both sexual and labor-related.

Budget and Energy Sector Development

Another issue delayed by the political crisis was the adoption of a 2012 budget. A $100 billion budget was adopted by the cabinet in December 2011, and it was adopted by the COR on

February 24, 2012. It is based on an $85 price for a barrel of oil, and, with prices about that level, the budget will likely be close to balanced. (The cabinet budget predicted a $10 billion deficit.)

About 90% of Iraq's budget is derived from oil export revenues, meaning that developing its energy sector is crucial to its financial future. Iraq possesses a proven 143 billion barrels of oil, and increasing exports should enable Iraq's GDP to grow by about 12% in 2012, according to the World Bank. After remaining well below the levels achieved prior to the ouster of Saddam Hussein, Iraq's oil exports recovered to about 2.1 million barrels per day by March 2012, roughly the level achieved during Saddam's rule. Production reached the milestone 3 million barrels per day mark in February 2012, which Iraqi leaders trumpeted as a key milestone in Iraq's recovery, and expanded further to about 3.2 million barrels per day in September 2012. Iraqi leaders say they want to increase production to over 10 million barrels per day by 2017, although then Ambassador-nominee McGurk testified on June 6, 2012, that the United States believes they'll achieve about half that level—about 5 million barrels per day by 2017. Iraq sold $17 billion worth of oil and related products during 2011.

What is helping the Iraqi production is the involvement of foreign firms, including BP, Exxon-Mobil, Occidental, and Chinese firms. U.S. firms assisted Iraq's export capacity by developing single-point mooring oil loading terminals to compensate for deterioration in Iraq's existing oil export infrastructure in Basra and Umm Qasr.

The growth of oil exports appears to be fueling a rapid expansion of the consumer sector. Press reports in 2012 have noted the development of several upscale malls and other consequences of positive economic progress.

Response to Arab Spring-Related Demonstrations

Iraq's government, although flawed, is the product of democratic choices. Therefore, many experts were surprised when protests (which built to the point where they ousted leaders in Egypt and Tunisia) began in several provinces of Iraq on February 6, 2011, and later expanded to numerous provinces. Twenty Iraqis were killed by security forces in the February 25, 2011, "Day of Rage" demonstrations called by Iraqi activists. However, although to some extent inspired by the uprisings throughout the Middle East, the Iraqi demonstrations did not have the similar objective of toppling Iraq's leadership.

Still, the spread of unrest into Iraq suggested to many that Iraqis have been frustrated by what they perceive as a nearly exclusive focus of the major factions on politics rather than governing or improving services. Many protesters expressed particular outrage at the still severe shortages of electricity in Iraq, as well as the lack of job opportunities and perceived elite corruption. Iraqis who cannot afford their own generators (or to share a generator with a few others) face repeated power outages every day. Many of the protests that took place were instigated by the Sadr faction, which sought to capitalize politically on governmental failures. The demonstrations caused the resignations of provincial governors in Wasit and Basra provinces and of several municipal leaders in Anbar Province. In sympathy with the protests, Jafar Al Sadr, who obtained the second-most votes in the March 2010 elections on Maliki's list (after Maliki himself), resigned from the COR on February 17, 2011.

Unrest in the KRG region appeared to reflect deep frustrations and was more intense than in the rest of Iraq. The unrest in Sulaymaniyah resulted in the deaths of at least three protestors at the hands of *peshmerga* and Kurdish intelligence (*Asayesh*), and was said to rattle the top Kurdish leaders, who fear the KRG's image as an oasis of stability and prosperity was clouded. Demonstrations in Sulaymaniyah on February 17, 2011, also revived long-standing but suppressed tensions between the PUK and the KDP as the KDP retaliated for protester attacks on some of its offices.

Protest-Prompted Governmental Reforms

The government was able to defuse popular unrest with varied measures. In February 2011, Maliki announced a voluntary cut in his salary (from about $350,000 per year to half that) and indicated he would not seek a third term when his current term expires in 2014. On February 27, 2011, he announced that his new cabinet would have "100 days" to prove its effectiveness or face replacement. That deadline expired on June 7, 2011, without significant incident, although U.S. diplomats say the government began public works projects and provided some fuel supplies as part of its efforts to show results by that time. In addition, on May 31, 2011, third deputy president Adel Abdul Mahdi resigned in an effort to show that the government is committed to cutting its bloated bureaucracy. To reinforce that commitment, the COR voted on July 30, 2011, to back Maliki's plan to reduce the number of cabinet posts from the current 42 to 29.

Another component of the response was to appoint several technocrats to permanently fill cabinet slots in ministries that deliver services to the public. In a wave of appointments on February 13, 2011, an Iraqiyya technocrat, Raad Shallal, was appointed minister of electricity and power. In addition, Municipality and Public Works Minister Adel Mohder was named, as were appointments to be ministers of state for tribal affairs, civilian community affairs, and national reconciliation. Shallal was removed in August 2011, most likely as a scapegoat for continued electricity shortages, although the stated cause of his removal was a failure to follow proper procedures in signing $1.7 billion worth of power plant construction contracts with Canadian and German firms.

In early June 2011, in advance of the June 7 "100 day" deadline, the government detained several dozen activists in order to preempt protests. Additional steps were taken subsequently to curb protests, including tolerating pro-government thugs to beat demonstrators on June 10, 2011. Either because of the repression or because of lack of popular support, subsequent demonstrations have been scattered and small.

General Human Rights Issues

U.S. and international officials say they expect the 2010-2014 government to make further progress establishing rule of law and adherence to international standards of human rights. The State Department's report on human rights for 2011 released May 24, 2012, largely repeated the previous years' criticisms of Iraq's human rights record and the attribution of deficiencies in human rights practices to the overall security situation and sectarian and factional divisions.[24] The State Department report cited a wide range of human rights problems committed by Iraqi government security and law enforcement personnel, including some unlawful killings; torture and other cruel punishments; poor conditions in prison facilities; denial of fair public trials; arbitrary arrest; arbitrary interference with privacy and home; limits on freedoms of speech, assembly, and association due to sectarianism and extremist threats; lack of protection of stateless

---

[24] http://www.state.gov/j/drl/rls/hrrpt/humanrightsreport/index.htm?dynamic_load_id=186428#wrapper

persons; wide scale governmental corruption; human trafficking; and limited exercise of labor rights. Many of these same abuses and deficiencies are discussed in the Human Rights Watch World Report for 2012, released January 22, 2012.

Trafficking in Persons

The State Department's Trafficking in Persons report for 2012, released on June 19, 2012, places Iraq in "Tier 2 Watch List" for the fourth year in a row. This is one rank short of Tier 3, the lowest ranking. For 2012, Iraq received a waiver from automatic downgrading to Tier 3 (which happens if a country is "watchlisted" for three straight years) because it has a plan to make significant efforts to meet minimum standards for the elimination of trafficking and is devoting significant resources to that plan.

Media and Free Expression

While State Department and other reports attribute most of Iraq's human rights difficulties to the security situation and factional infighting, apparent curbs on free expression appear independent of such factors. One issue that troubles human rights activists is a law, passed by the COR in August 2011, called the "Journalist Rights Law." The law purports to protect journalists but left many of the provisions of Saddam-era libel and defamation laws in place. For example, the new law leaves in place imprisonment for publicly insulting the government. The State Department human rights report for 2011 noted continuing instances of harassment and intimidation of journalists who write about corruption and the lack of government services. Much of the private media that operate is controlled by individual factions or powerful personalities. There are no overt government restrictions on access to the Internet.

In March 2012, some observers reported a setback to free expression, although instigated by militias or non-governmental groups, not the government. There were reports of 14 youths having been stoned to death by militiamen for wearing Western-style clothes and haircuts collectively known as "Emo" style. In late June 2012, the government ordered the closing of 44 new organizations that it said were operating without a license. Included in the closure list were the BBC, Voice of America, and the U.S.-funded Radio Sawa. The COR is also in the process of considering an "Information Crimes Law" to regulate the use of information networks, computers, and other electronic devices and systems. Human Rights Watch said in July 2012 that the draft law "violates international standards protecting due process, freedom of speech, and freedom of association."[25]

Labor Rights

A 1987 (Saddam era) labor code remains in effect, restricting many labor rights, particularly in the public sector. Although the 2005 constitution provides for the right to strike and form unions, the labor code virtually rules out independent union activity. Unions have no legal power to negotiate with employers or protect workers' rights through collective bargaining.

---

[25] Human Rights Watch. "Iraq's Information Crimes Law: Badly Written Provisions and Draconian Punishments Violate due Process and Free Speech." July 12, 2012.

Religious Freedom/Situation of the Christian Religious Minority

The issue of religious freedom in Iraq tends to center on government treatment of religious minorities. However, conservative Shiite and Sunni clerics seek to enforce aspects of Islamic law and customs, sometimes coming into conflict with Iraq's generally secular traditions. Reflecting the conservative Islamic attitudes of many Iraqis, on September 13, 2012, hundreds—presumably Shiites—took to the streets in predominantly Shiite Sadr City to protest the "Innocence of Muslims" video that was produced in the United States and set off protests throughout the Middle East in September 2012.

As far as treatment of religious minorities, a major concern is the safety and security of Iraq's Christian and other religious minority populations (Yazidis, Shabaks, Sabeans, for example), which are concentrated in northern Iraq as well as in Baghdad. Since the 2003 U.S. intervention, more than half of the 1 million-1.5 million Christian population that was there during Saddam's time have left. Recent estimates indicate that the Christian population of Iraq is less than 500,000.

The current situation of Christians and other religious minorities is addressed in the State Department's "July–December 2010 Religious Freedom Report," released September 13, 2011. The report noted "no change" in the status of respect for religious freedom by the government for the reporting period, but did list numerous attacks on the community's houses of worship and its clergy. The report praised the COR's November 2010 approval of a document calling on the government to protect Iraq's Christians.

Attacks on members of the community appear to occur in waves. The body of Chaldean Catholic archbishop Faraj Rahho was discovered in Mosul on March 13, 2008, two weeks after his reported kidnapping. An attack on the Yazidis in August 2007, which killed about 500 people, appeared to exemplify the precarious situation for Iraqi minorities. In the run-up to the January 2009 provincial elections, about 1,000 Christian families reportedly fled the province in October 2008, although Iraqi officials report that most families returned by December 2008. The issue faded in 2009 but then resurfaced late in that year when about 10,000 Christians in northern Iraq, fearing bombings and intimidation, fled the areas near Kirkuk during October-December 2009. On October 31, 2010, a major attack on Christians occurred when a church in Baghdad (Sayidat al-Najat Church) was besieged by militants and as many as 60 worshippers were killed. The siege shook the faith of the Christian community in their security. Many Christian families fled their homes after the church attack, often going to live with relatives in Christian-inhabited locations around Iraq. Partly as a result, Christian celebrations of Christmas 2010 were said to be subdued—following three years in which Christians had felt confident enough to celebrate that holiday openly. Several other attacks appearing to target Iraqi Christians have taken place since.

Some Iraqi Christians blame all the various attacks on them on Al Qaeda in Iraq, which is still somewhat strong in Nineveh Province and which associates Christians with the United States. Some human rights groups allege that it is the Kurds who are committing abuses against Christians and other minorities in the Nineveh Plains, close to the KRG-controlled region. Kurdish leaders deny the allegations, and the State Department human rights report for 2010 says the KRG has permitted Christians fleeing violence in Baghdad to relocate into KRG-controlled areas. Some Iraqi Christian groups advocate a "Nineveh Plains Province Solution," in which the Nineveh Plains would be turned into a self-administering region, possibly its own province but affiliated or under KRG control. Supporters of the idea claim such a zone would pose no threat to the integrity of Iraq, but others say the plan's inclusion of a separate Christian security force could set the scene for violence and confrontation. Even at the height of the U.S. military presence in Iraq, U.S. forces did not specifically protect Christian sites at all times, partly because Christian leaders do not want to appear closely allied with the United States.

The FY2008 consolidated appropriation earmarked $10 million in ESF from previous appropriations to assist the Nineveh Plain Christians. A supplemental appropriation for 2008 and 2009 (P.L. 110-252) earmarked another $10 million for this purpose. The Consolidated Appropriations Act of 2010 (P.L. 111-117) made a similar provision for FY2010, although focused on Middle East minorities generally and without a specific dollar figure mandated for Iraqi Christians. In the 112th Congress, a bill, H.R. 440, which would establish a post of Special Envoy to promote religious freedom in the Middle East and South Central Asia, passed the House on July 29, 2011, by a vote of 402-20. Ambassador-designate to Iraq, Robert Stephen Beecroft, testified at his Senate Foreign Relations Committee confirmation hearings on September 19, 2012 that the State Department has spent $72 million total to protect religious minorities in Iraq.

Women's Rights

Iraq has a tradition of secularism and liberalism, and women's rights issues have not been as large a concern for international observers and rights groups as they have in Afghanistan or the Persian Gulf states, for example. Women serve at many levels of government, as discussed above, and are well integrated into the work force in all types of jobs and professions. By tradition, many Iraqi women wear traditional coverings but many adopt Western dress. On October 6, 2011, the COR passed legislation to lift Iraq's reservation to Article 9 of the Convention on the Elimination of All Forms of Discrimination Against Women.

Corruption

The State Department human rights report for 2011 contains substantial detail on the continuing lack of progress in curbing governmental corruption. The report discusses political and other factors that have caused anti-corruption institutions, such as the Commission on Integrity (COI) and the Joint Anti-Corruption Council, to be regularly thwarted or hampered in attempts to investigate and prosecute corruption. The Joint Anti-Corruption Council is tasked with implementing the government's 2010-14 Anti-Corruption Strategy. The State Department report states, in a three month period in 2011, over 200 corruption investigations were halted on the authority of Iraqi ministers—presumably because they did not want their departments or poltical allies investigated. The COR has its own Integrity Committee that oversees the executive branch and the governmental anti-corruption bodies. And, the KRG has its own separate anti-corruption institutions, including an Office of Governance and Integrity in the KRG council of ministers.

Executions

The death penalty is legal in Iraq. On August 28, 2012, the government executed 21 people, including three women, convicted of terrorism-related charges. Earlier, in June 2012, Amnesty International condemned the "alarming" increase in executions, which had by then put 70 persons to death. U.N. High Commissioner for Human Rights Navi Pillay also expressed shock in 2012 over the high number of executions in Iraq.

Mass Graves

As is noted in the State Department report on human rights for 2010, the Iraqi government continues to uncover mass graves of victims of the Saddam regime. This effort is under the authority of the Human Rights Ministry. On April 15, 2011, a mass grave of more than 800 bodies became the latest such discovery. The largest to date was a mass grave in Mahawil, near Hilla, that contained 3,000 bodies; the grave was discovered in 2003, shortly after the fall of the regime.

Regional Dimension

For Iraq's neighbors as well as for the United States, the stakes in the outcome of the political process in Iraq have been high. Still at odds with Iran on virtually every issue in the Middle East, the United States has considerable concerns about the potential for increased Iranian influence in Iraq now that U.S. forces are no longer there. Yet, Iraq appears to seek primarily to reintegrate into the Arab fold—of which Iran is not a part—after more than 20 years of ostracism following Iraq's invasion of Kuwait in August 1990. That motive mitigates, to some extent, Iranian influence in Iraq because the Arab world is primarily composed of Sunni Muslims and much of the Arab world is either at odds with or highly suspicious of Iran. Still, Iraq's close relations with Iran has contributed to Iraq's taking a different position on Syria than most of its Arab neighbors, thus hindering Iraq's Arab reintegration.

Iraq's reintegration into the Arab fold took a large step forward with the holding of an Arab League summit in Baghdad during March 27-29, 2012. Iraq hailed the gathering as a success primarily because of the absence of major security incidents during the gathering. However, only 9 heads of state out of the 22 Arab League members attended, and only one Persian Gulf leader, Amir Sabah al-Ahmad Al Sabah of Kuwait, attended. Building on that success, and on its relations with both the United States and Iran, on May 23-24, 2012, Iraq hosted nuclear talks between Iran and the six negotiating powers (United States, Britain, France, Germany, Russia, and China).

Iraq is also sufficiently confident to begin offering assistance to other emerging Arab democracies. Utilizing its base of expertise in chemical weaponry during the Saddam Hussein regime, Iraq has provided some technical assistance to the post-Qadhafi authorities in Libya to help them clean up chemical weapons stockpiles built up by the Qadhafi regime. It has also donated $100,000 and provided advisers to support elections in Tunisia after its 2011 revolution.[26]

Iran

Despite Iraq's attempts to rebuild bridges in the Arab world, some argue that the withdrawal of all U.S. troops from Iraq represented a success for Iranian strategy and that Iranian influence in Iraq is preponderant. Others argue that U.S. policy created the ideal opportunity for Iran's exercise of influence in Iraq by bringing to power in Iraq, through election, Shiite Islamist politicians long linked to Iran.

---

[26] Tim Arango. "Iraq Election Official's Arrest Casts Doubt on Prospects for Fair Voting." *New York Times*, April 17, 2012.

To counter the impression that Iran might benefit from the complete U.S. pullout, Secretary of State Clinton said on October 23, 2011, that:

> I think Iran should look at the region. We may not be leaving military bases in Iraq, but we have bases elsewhere. We have support and training assets elsewhere. We have a NATO ally in Turkey. The United States is very present in the region.

That theme was echoed by Secretary of Defense Leon Panetta. That same day, he said Iraq, even without U.S. troops present there, would be able to counter any threat from Iranian influence or from Iran-backed Iraqi Shiite militias. These militias have been perceived as a threat particularly to U.S. personnel in southern Iraq, although that threat reportedly has abated since early 2012.

Prime Minister Maliki has tried to calm fears that Iran exercises undue influence over post-U.S. military Iraq. In so doing, he has stressed themes that are advanced by many experts that Iraqi nationalism is resisting Iranian influence. Experts also note lingering distrust of Iran from the 1980-1988 Iran-Iraq war, in which an estimated 300,000 Iraqi military personnel (Shiite and Sunni) died. In his December 5, 2011, op-ed in the *Washington Post*, entitled "Building a Stable Iraq," Maliki wrote:

> Iraq is a sovereign country. Our foreign policy is rooted in the fact that we do not interfere in the affairs of other countries; accordingly, we oppose foreign interference in Iraqi affairs.

Defense and security ties between Iran and Iraq have been forecast but little has materialized. In an interview with CNN broadcast on October 23, 2011, Iran's President Mahmoud Ahmadinejad said Iran planned a closer security relationship with Iraqi forces after U.S. troops depart. In the days after the U.S. withdrawal that was completed December 18, 2011, Iran announced it would welcome closer defense ties to Iraq, including training Iraqi forces, although no such training has been reported to date. However, in May 2012, Iraqi courts acquitted and Iraq released from prison a purported Hezbollah commander, Ali Musa Daqduq, although he reportedly remains under house arrest. He had been in U.S. custody for alleged activities against U.S. forces but, under the U.S.-Iraq Security Agreement (discussed below) he was transferred to Iraqi custody in December 2011. In July 2012, U.S. officials asked Iraqi leaders to review the Daqduq case or extradite him to the United States.

Iraq's Shiite clerics also resist Iranian interference and take pride in Najaf as a more prominent center of Shiite theology and history than is the Iranian holy city of Qom. In late 2011, representatives of Ayatollah Mahmud Shahrudi, an Iraqi cleric long resident in Iraq, opened offices in Najaf, Iraq. This was widely seen as an effort to promote Shahrudi as a possible successor as *marja taqlid* ("source of inspiration,"—the most senior Shiite cleric) to the increasingly frail Grand Ayatollah Ali al-Sistani. During an April 22-23, 2012, visit to Iran, Maliki met with Shahrudi, in addition to meeting senior Iranian figures. However, observers say the offices have not created a wave of support for Shahrudi as successor to Sistani.

Some assess that evidence of Iranian influence can be seen in Iraq's alignment, in general, with Iranian policy that seeks to keep Bashar Al Assad in power in Syria. This has put Iraq in a difficult position between its two allies, the United States and Iran, in that the United States seeks Assad's ouster and is demanding Iraq not cooperate with any Iranian efforts to keep Assad in power. This is discussed further below.

Still others see Iranian influence as less political than economic, raising questions about whether Iran is using Iraq to try to avoid the effects of international sanctions. Some reports say Iraq is cooperating with the Iranian efforts, allowing it to interact with Iraq's energy sector and its banking system. In July 2012, the Treasury Dept. imposed sanctions on the Elaf Islamic Bank of Iraq for allegedly conducting financial transactions with the Iranian banking system that violated the Comprehensive Iran Sanctions, Accountability, and Divestment Act of 2012 (CISADA, P.L. 111-915). On the other hand, in at least one way Iraq is assisting U.S. policy toward Iran by supplying oil customers who, in cooperation with U.S. sanctions against Iran, are cutting back buys of oil from Iran. Observers also report that Iran is heavily promoting brands of its products, such as yogurt and jams, in Iraqi shops primarily in southern Iraq. Some Iraqi businessmen are said to resent what they believe is Iranian dumping of cheap products in Iraq, which is depressing the development of Iraqi industries. Iranian officials said in mid-September 2012 that Iran's exports to Iraq will reach about $10 billion from March 2012-March 2013, a large increase from the $7 billion in exports in the prior one year.

Iranian Opposition: People's Mojahedin/Camp Ashraf and PJAK

The Iraqi government treatment of the population of Camp Ashraf, a camp in which over 3,500 Iranian oppositionists (People's Mojahedin Organization of Iran, PMOI) have resided, is an indicator of the government's close ties to Iran. The residents of the camp accuse the government of repression and of scheming to expel the residents or extradite them to Iran, where they might face prosecution or death. An Iraqi military redeployment at the camp on April 8, 2011, resulted in major violence against camp residents in which 36 of them were killed.

In November 2011, Maliki insisted that camp will close at the end of 2011, and the U.N. High Commissioner for Refugees, the European Union, and other organizations worked to broker a solution that avoids violence or forcible expulsion. In late December 2011 Maliki signed an agreement with the United Nations on December 26, 2011, to relocate the population to former U.S. military base Camp Liberty. The PMOI later accepted the agreement, dropping demands that U.S. troops guard the residents during any relocation, and all but a residual 200 Ashraf residents have completed their relocation to a former U.S. base, Camp Liberty (renamed Camp Hurriya). There, each case is being evaluated by the U.N. High Commissioner for Refugees for the potential for relocation outside Iraq. The relocation was a major factor in the U.S. decision, formalized on September 28, 2012, to take the PMOI off the U.S. list of Foreign Terrorist Organizations. This issue is discussed in substantially greater detail in CRS Report RL32048, *Iran: U.S. Concerns and Policy Responses*, by Kenneth Katzman.

Iran has periodically acted against other Iranian opposition groups based in Iraq. The Free Life Party (PJAK) consists of Iranian Kurds, and it is allied with the Kurdistan Workers' Party that opposes the government of Turkey. Iran has shelled purported camps of the group on several occasions. Iran is also reportedly attempting to pressure the bases and offices in Iraq of such Iranian Kurdish parties as the Kurdistan Democratic Party of Iran (KDP-I) and Komaleh.

Syria

As noted above, Iraq has been viewed as unhelpful to U.S. policy toward Syria—which is to oust President Bashar Al Assad—in large part because Maliki's government sees the likely next rulers of Syria will almost certainly be Sunni Arabs. Syria would then likely align with Saudi Arabia, Turkey, and Jordan, and become less friendly to Iraq than Assad is now. During March 2011-August 2011, Iraq, as did Iran, refrained from sharp criticism of Assad for using military force against protests. During that same period, Maliki received high-level business and other delegations from Syria in a show of support for his government. In September 2011 Iraq moved closer to the Iranian position by calling on Assad to make major reforms or risk unrest that could spill into Iraq itself. Iraq opposed the 22-country Arab League move in November 2011 to suspend Syria's membership—although it formally abstained on the vote, with Yemen and Lebanon the only two "no" votes. But, suggesting it believes Assad might fall, Iraq voted for a January 22, 2012, Arab League plan for a transition of power in Syria. Foreign Minister Hoshyar Zebari has attended U.S.-led meetings of "Friends of Syria" countries that are seeking Assad's ouster.

A major issue that has erupted between Iraq and the United States in August and September 2012 is Iraq's reported permission for Iranian arms supplies to overfly Iraq en route to Syria.[27] Iraq had been preventing them as of March 2012 but the flights reportedly resumed in August 2012. Following high level U.S. demands that Iraq request the Iranian flights land in Iraq for inspection, Iraq stopped a North Korean flight to Syria on September 21, 2012 and announced on September 30 that it would conduct random searches of Iranian overflights. The first such search of an Iranian flight was conducted on October 2, 2012, but it was allowed to proceed when no arms were found aboard.

Aside from official Iraqi policy, the unrest in Syria has generated a scramble among Iraqi factions to affect the outcome there. As discussed above, AQ-I members have reportedly entered Syria to help the mostly Sunni opposition to President Assad. The Iraqi government announced in February 2012 that it was tightening its border with Syria to prevent the movement of Iraqi militants and arms into Syria. The KRG appears to be assisting the Syrian Kurds, who joined the revolt against Assad in July 2012. KRG President Barzani has hosted several meetings of Syrian Kurds to promote unity and a common strategy among them.

Turkey

Turkey's concerns focus mostly, although not exclusively, on northern Iraq, which borders Turkey. Turkey has historically been viewed as concerned about the Iraqi Kurdish insistence on autonomy and Iraqi Kurds' ethnically based sympathies for Kurdish oppositionists in Turkey. The anti-Turkey Kurdistan Workers' Party (PKK) has long maintained camps inside Iraq, along the border with Turkey. Turkey continues to conduct periodic bombardments and other military operations against the PKK encampments in Iraq. For example, in October 2011, Turkey sent ground troops into northern Iraq to attack PKK bases following the killing of 24 Turkish soldiers by the PKK. However, suggesting that it has built a pragmatic relationship with the KRG, Turkey has emerged as the largest outside investor in northern Iraq and is building an increasingly close political relationship with the KRG as well.

Relations between Turkey and the Iraqi government have worsened since the beginning of 2012 because of Vice President Tariq al-Hashimi's refuge there. Maliki and his allies sought his extradition for trial, but Turkey has not turned him over. On August 2, 2012, Turkish Foreign Minister Ahmet Davotoglu visited the city of Kirkuk, prompting a rebuke from Iraq's Foreign Ministry that the visit constituted inappropriate interference in Iraqi affairs.

---

[27] Kristina Wong, " Iraq Resists U.S. Prod, Lets Iran Fly Arms to Syria." *Washington Times*, March 16, 2012.

Gulf States

Iraq also has unresolved disputes with several of the Sunni-led Persian Gulf states who have not fully accommodated themselves to the fact that Iraq is now dominated by Shiite factions. However, Iraq has tried, with some success, to settle some of these issues to encourage maximum Gulf participation in the March 27-29, 2012, Arab League summit in Baghdad. All the Gulf states were represented at the summit but, among Gulf rulers, only Amir Sabah of Kuwait attended. Qatar sent a very low-level delegation which it said openly was meant as a protest against the Iraqi government's treatment of Sunni Arab factions.

Saudi Arabia had been widely criticized by Iraqi leaders because it has not opened an embassy in Baghdad, a move Saudi Arabia pledged in 2008 and which the United States has long urged. This issue was mitigated on February 20, 2012, when Saudi Arabia announced that it had named its ambassador to Jordan, Fahd al-Zaid, to serve as a non-resident ambassador to Iraq concurrently. However, it did not announce the opening of an embassy in Baghdad. The Saudi move came after a visit by Iraqi national security officials to Saudi Arabia to discuss greater cooperation on counterterrorism and the fate of about 400 Arab prisoners in Iraqi jails. The other Gulf countries have opened embassies and all except the UAE have appointed full ambassadors to Iraq.

The relationship with Kuwait has always been considered difficult to resolve because of the legacy of the 1990 Iraqi invasion. However, a possible indication of greater acceptance of the Iraqi government by the state it once occupied (1990-1991) came when Kuwait's prime minister visited Iraq on January 12, 2011. Maliki subsequently visited Kuwait on February 16, 2011. These key exchanges took place after the U.N. Security Council on December 15, 2010, passed three resolutions (1956, 1957, and 1958) that had the net effect of lifting most Saddam-era sanctions on Iraq, although the U.N.-run reparations payments process remains intact (and deducts 5% from Iraq's total oil revenues). A U.N. envoy, Gennadi Tarasov, remains empowered by the Security Council to clear up the issues of Kuwaitis and other nationals missing from the Iraqi invasion of Kuwait, and the issue of the missing Kuwaiti national archives that Iraq allegedly took out of Kuwait. Very little progress on these issues has been made in recent years, as was made clear in a Security Council statement of December 15, 2011 (SC/10490). Other mutual suspicions persist—in August 2011 Iraqi politicians accused Kuwait of intruding on Iraq's oil through slant drilling at the border.

Some of these unresolved issues moved forward during the March 15, 2012, visit of Maliki to Kuwait. After Maliki's meetings, the two announced that Iraq had agreed to pay its share of compensation to maintain border markings between the two. Iraq agreed to pay $300 million to the Kuwaiti government and to invest $200 million in a joint venture of the two as settlement for Kuwait Airways' claim for $1.2 billion in compensation for planes and parts allegedly stolen by Iraq during the 1990-1991 occupation. These agreements paved the way for Amir Sabah to attend the Arab League summit in Baghdad. Subsequently, Iraq-Kuwait direct flights resumed, and an agreement was reached for Iraq to pay its share of the costs of maintaining border markings.

The government of Bahrain, which is mostly Sunni, also fears that Iraq might work to empower Shiite oppositionists who have demonstrated for a constitutional monarchy during 2011. Ayatollah Sistani is revered by many Bahraini Shiites, and Iraqi Shiites have demonstrated in solidarity with the Bahraini opposition, but there is no evidence that Iraq has had any direct role in the Bahrain unrest.

U.S. Military Withdrawal and Post-2011 Policy

A complete U.S. military withdrawal from Iraq by the end of 2011 was a specific stipulation of the November 2008 U.S.-Iraq Security Agreement (SA), which took effect on January 1, 2009. Following the SA's entry into force, President Obama, on February 27, 2009, outlined a U.S. troop drawdown plan that provided for a drawdown of U.S. combat brigades by the end of August 2010, with a residual force of 50,000 primarily for training the Iraq Security Forces, to remain until the end of 2011. An interim benchmark in the SA was the June 30, 2009, withdrawal of U.S. combat troops from Iraq's cities. These withdrawal deadlines were strictly adhered to.

Question of Whether U.S. Forces Would Remain Beyond 2011

During 2011, with the deadline for a complete U.S. withdrawal approaching, continuing high-profile attacks, fears of expanded Iranian influence, and perceived deficiencies in Iraq's nearly 700,000 member security forces caused U.S. officials to seek to revise the SA to keep some U.S. troops in Iraq after 2011. Some U.S. experts feared the rifts among major ethnic and sectarian communities were still wide enough that Iraq could still become a "failed state" unless some U.S. troops remained—although U.S. officials emphasized that their ongoing concerns about the ISF centered on Iraq's ability to defend its airspace and borders. Iraqi comments, such as an October 30, 2011, statement by Iraqi Army Chief of Staff Lieutenant General Babaker Zebari to the effect that Iraq would be unable to execute full external defense until 2020-2024, reinforced those who asserted that a U.S. force presence was still needed.[28] Renegotiating the SA to allow for a continued U.S. troop presence required discussions with the Iraqi government and a ratification vote of the Iraqi COR.

Several high-level U.S. visits and statements urged the Iraqis to consider extending the U.S. troop presence. Maliki told visiting Speaker of the House John Boehner, during an April 16, 2011, visit to Baghdad, that Iraqi forces were capable of securing Iraq after 2011, but that Iraq would welcome U.S. training and arms after that time.[29] Subsequent to Boehner's visit, Maliki, anticipating that a vote of the COR would be needed for any extension, stated that a request for U.S. troops might be made if there were a "consensus" among political blocs, which he defined as at least 70% concurrence.[30] This appeared to be an effort to isolate the Sadr faction, which was the most vocal opponent of a continuing U.S. presence.

In his first visit to Iraq as Defense Secretary on July 11, 2011, Leon Panetta urged Iraqi leaders to make an affirmative decision, and soon. On August 3, 2011, major factions gave Maliki their backing to negotiate an SA extension, and Secretary Panetta said on August 20, 2011, that it was likely that Iraq would request a continued U.S. presence primarily to train the ISF. In September 2011, a figure of about 15,000 remaining U.S. troops, reflecting recommendations of the U.S. military, was being widely discussed.[31] However, the issue became a subject of substantial debate when the *New York Times* reported on September 7, 2011, that the Administration was considering

---

[28] "Iraq General Says Forces Not Ready 'Until 2020.'" Agence France Presse, October 30, 2011.

[29] Prashant Rao. "Maliki Tells US' Boehner Iraqi Troops Are Ready." *Agence France Presse*, April 16, 2011.

[30] Aaron Davis. "Maliki Seeking Consensus on Troops." *Washington Post*, May 12, 2011.

[31] Author conversations with Iraq experts in Washington, DC, 2011.

proposing to Iraq to retain only about 3,000-4,000 forces, mostly in a training role, after 2011.[32] Many experts and some Members of Congress criticized that figure as too low to ensure force protection and carry out the intended missions.

President Obama Announces Decision on Full Withdrawal

The difficulty in the negotiations—primarily a function of strident Sadrist opposition to a continued U.S. presence—became clearer on October 5, 2011, when Iraq issued a statement that some U.S. military personnel should remain in Iraq as trainers but that Iraq would not extend the legal protections contained in the existing SA. That stipulation failed to meet the requirements of the Defense Department, which feared that trying any American soldier under the Iraqi constitution could lead to serious crises at some stage.

On October 21, 2011, President Obama announced that the United States and Iraq had agreed that, in accordance with the November 2008 Security Agreement (SA) with Iraq, all U.S. troops would leave Iraq at the end of 2011. With the formal end of the U.S. combat mission on August 31, 2010, U.S. forces dropped to 47,000, and force levels dropped steadily from August to December 2011. The last U.S. troop contingent crossed into Kuwait on December 18, 2011.

The withdrawal—and perhaps the political crisis that broke out immediately after the completion of the withdrawal—caused some to argue that U.S. gains were jeopardized and that the Administration should have pressed Iraqi leaders harder to allow a U.S. contingent to remain. Those who support the Administration view say that political crisis was likely no matter when the United States withdrew and that it is the responsibility of the Iraqis to resolve their differences.

Structure of the Post-Troop Relationship

After the withdrawal announcement, senior U.S. officials, including Defense Secretary Leon Panetta, stated that the United States would be able to continue to help Iraq secure itself using programs commonly used with other countries. Administration officials stressed that the U.S. political and residual security-related presence would be sufficient to exert influence and leverage to ensure that Iraq remained stable, allied to the United States, continuing to move toward full democracy, and economically growing and vibrant.

At the time of the withdrawal, there were about 16,000 total U.S. personnel in Iraq, about half of which were contractors. Of the contractors, most are security contractors protecting the U.S. Embassy and consulates, and other State Department and Office of Security Cooperation-Iraq facilities throughout Iraq. However, staff cuts discussed below have left the total number of U.S. personnel in Iraq at about 12,500 as of the end of June 2012.

Office of Security Cooperation-Iraq (OSC-I)

The Office of Security Cooperation—Iraq (OSC-I), operating under the authority of the U.S. Ambassador to Iraq, is the primary Iraq-based U.S. institution that continues to train and mentor the Iraqi military. It is funded with the Foreign Military Financing (FMF) funds discussed in the aid table below. OSC-I is the largest U.S. security cooperation office in the world. It works out of

---

[32] Eric Schmitt and Steven Lee Myers. "Plan Would Keep Military in Iraq Beyond Deadline." September 7, 2011.

the U.S. Embassy in Baghdad and five other locations around Iraq (Kirkuk Regional Airport Base, Tikrit, Besmaya, Umm Qasr, and Taji), but OSC-I plans to transfer its facilities to the Iraqi government by the end of 2013.

The total OCS-I personnel numbers over 3,500, but the vast majority are security and support personnel, most of which are contractors. Of the staff, about 175 are U.S. military personnel and an additional 45 are Defense Department civilians. About 46 of the staff administers the Foreign Military Sales (FMS) program and other security assistance programs such as the International Military Education and Training (IMET) program. Since 2005, DOD has administered 231 U.S.-funded FMS cases totaling $2.5 billion, and 201 Iraq-funded cases totaling $7.9 billion.

The largest FMS case is the sale of 36 U.S.-made F-16 combat aircraft to Iraq, notified to Congress in two equal tranches, the latest of which was made on December 12, 2011 (Transmittal No. 11-46). The total value of the sale of 36 F-16s is up to $6.5 billion when all parts, training, and weaponry are included. Iraq has paid $2.5 billion of that amount, to date. The first deliveries of the aircraft are scheduled for September 2014.

Another large part of the arms sale program to Iraq is for 140 M1A1 Abrams tanks. Deliveries began in August 2010 and the last of them were delivered in late August 2012. the tanks cost about $860 million, of which $800 million was paid out of Iraq's national funds.

In addition to administering arms sales to Iraq, OSC-I's mission is to conduct train and assist programs for the Iraq military. These personnel are to cooperate with Iraq's forces on counterterrorism, naval and air defense, and conduct joint exercises. It is envisioned that U.S. personnel will be "embedded" with Iraqi forces as trainers not only tactically, but at the institutional level by advising Iraqi security ministries and its command structure.

However, to date, these missions are not in effect because the United States and Iraq have not agreed on a document that outlines the responsibilities and size of these missions, and OSC-I personnel lack the ability to carry weapons inside Iraq. There is no currently operative Status of Forces Agreement (SOFA) with Iraq, which would be needed for combined joint exercises. In some cases, not limited to OSC-I personnel, Iraq has been detaining U.S. security contractors at checkpoints, complicating not only the U.S. security assistance effort but also the U.S. effort to protect its own personnel and facilities.

On October 2, 2012, OSC-I officials say they planned to review their operations because the Continuing Appropriations for FY2013 (P.L. 112-175), did not reauthorize—for FY2013 that began October 1—U.S. funding to train the ISF. Defense Department spokespersons said they are reviewing the availability of other authorities that would authorize OSC-I training activities in Iraq.

Police Development Program

A separate program is the Police Development Program, which is the largest program that has transitioned from DOD to State Department lead. An October 2011 audit by the SIGIR (Special Inspector General for Iraq Reconstruction) identified deficiencies in the U.S.-funded training program for the Iraqi police forces (Police Development Program, PDP) as that responsibility was transferred from DOD to State on October 1, 2011.[33] That program draws on International Narcotics and Law Enforcement (INCLE) funds. However, Iraq's drive to emerge from U.S. tutelage has produced apparent Iraqi disinterest in the PDP. It now consists of only 36 advisers, about 10% of what was envisioned as an advisory force of 350. Two facilities built with over $200 million in U.S. funds (Baghdad Police College Annex and part of the U.S. consulate in Basra) are to be turned over the Iraqi government by December 2012. Some press reports say there is Administration consideration of discontinuing the program entirely.[34]

Is Iraq Reconsidering Downplaying Security Programs?

The heightened AQ-I activity in summer 2012 may have shaken the Iraqi leadership's confidence in the ISF, and possibly prompted some rethinking of the disengagement with the OSC-I and PDP programs discussed above. On August 19, 2012, en route to a visit to Iraq, Chairman of the Joint Chiefs of Staff Gen. Martin Dempsey said that "I think [Iraqi leaders] recognize their capabilities may require yet more additional development and I think they're reaching out to us to see if we can help them with that." This could lead to an Iraqi rededication to the programs discussed above or it could lead to discussion of joint exercises with the United States and other U.S. training and security cooperation.[35]

Gen. Dempsey's August 21, 2012 visit focused on the security deterioration, as well as the Iranian overflights to Syria, according to press reports. Regarding U.S.-Iraq security relations, Iraq reportedly expressed interest in expanded U.S. training of the ISF as well as accelerated delivery of U.S. arms to be sold, including radar, air defense systems, and border security equipment.[36] Some refurbished air defense guns are being provided free of charge as excess defense articles (EDA), but Iraq was said to lament that the guns would not arrive until June 2013. Iraq reportedly argued that the equipment was needed to help it enforce insistence that Iranian overflights to Syria land in Iraq for inspection. It was subsequently reported that, at the request of Iraq, a unit of Army Special Operations forces had recently deployed to Iraq to advise on counterterrorism and help with intelligence, presumably against AQ-I.[37]

The Diplomatic and Economic Relationship

In his withdrawal announcement, President Obama stated that, through U.S. assistance programs, the United States would be able to continue to develop all facets of the bilateral relationship with Iraq and help strengthen its institutions."[38] The bilateral civilian relationship was the focus of a visit to Iraq by Vice President Biden in early December 2011, just prior to the December 12, 2011, Maliki visit to the United States, which reportedly focused on these issues but also exposed some U.S.-Iraq disagreements, such as over policy toward Syria.

The cornerstone of the bilateral relationship is the Strategic Framework Agreement (SFA). The SFA, signed and entered into effect at the same time as the SA, presents a framework for long-

---

[33] http://www.sigir.mil/files/audits/12-006.pdf#view=fit.

[34] Tim Arango. "U.S. May Scrap Costly Efforts to Train Iraqi Policy." *New York Times*, May 13, 2012.

[35] "U.S. Hopes For Stronger Military Ties With Iraq: General" Agence France-Presse, August 19, 2012.

[36] Dan De Luce. "U.S. 'Significant' in Iraq Despite Troop Exit: Dempsey." Agence France-Presse, August 21, 2012.

[37] Tim Arango. "Syrian Civil War Poses New Peril For Fragile Iraq." New York Times, September 25, 2012.

[38] Remarks by the President on Ending the War in Iraq." http://www.whitehouse.gov, October 21, 2011.

---

term U.S.-Iraqi relations, and is intended to help orient Iraq's politics and its economy toward the West and the developed nations, and reduce its reliance on Iran or other regional states.

The SFA provides for the following (among other provisions):

- U.S.-Iraq cooperation "based on mutual respect," and that the United States will not use Iraqi facilities to launch any attacks against third countries, and will not seek permanent bases.

- U.S support for Iraqi democracy and support for Iraq in regional and international organizations.

- U.S.-Iraqi dialogue to increase Iraq's economic development, including through the Dialogue on Economic Cooperation and a Trade and Investment Framework Agreement.

- Promotion of Iraq's development of its electricity, oil, and gas sector.

- U.S.-Iraq dialogue on agricultural issues and promotion of Iraqi participation in agricultural programs run by the U.S. Department of Agriculture and USAID.

- Cultural cooperation through several exchange programs, such as the Youth Exchange and Study Program and the International Visitor Leadership Program.

State Department-run aid programs are intended to fulfill the objectives of the SFA, according to State Department budget documents. These programs, implemented mainly through the Economic Support Fund account, and based on the State Department budget justification for foreign operations for FY2013, are intended to:

- Promote Iraqi political reconciliation and peaceful dispute resolution.

- Strengthen the ability of COR deputies to represent their constituents.

- Make the electoral institutions, such as the IHEC, more effective.

- Strengthen the delivery of services to citizens.

- Improve primary education.

- Assist local governing bodies, such as the provincial councils.

- Promote Iraqi economic growth and the development of the private sector, particularly the financial sector.

- Continue counterterrorism operations (NADR funds).

- Institute anti-corruption initiatives.

U.S. officials stress that the United States does not bear the only burden for implementing the programs above, in light of the fact that Iraq is now a major oil exporter. For programs run by USAID in Iraq, Iraq matches dollar for dollar the U.S. funding contribution.

The State Department as Lead Agency

Virtually all of the responsibility for conducting the bilateral relationship falls on the State Department, which became the lead U.S. agency in Iraq as of October 1, 2011. With the transition completed, the State Department announced on March 9, 2012, that its "Office of the Iraq

Transition Coordinator" has closed. In concert with that closure, the former coordinator, Ambassador Pat Haslach, assumed a senior post in another State Department bureau. Of the total U.S. personnel in Iraq, about 1,200 are U.S. diplomats or other civilian employees of the U.S. government.[39]

In July 2011, as part of the transition to State leadership in Iraq, the United States formally opened consulates in Basra, Irbil, and Kirkuk. An embassy branch office was considered for Mosul but cost and security issues have kept the U.S. facility there limited to a diplomatic office.

Not only have U.S. plans for some consulates been altered, but the size and cost of the U.S. civilian presence in Iraq is undergoing reduction. In part this is because Iraqi leaders chafe at further U.S. tutelage and advice, and are less welcoming of frequent U.S. diplomatic visits. Press reports say the Iraqis are increasingly displacing foreign firms and contractors from the International Zone (Green Zone) in favor of Iraqi institutions, and U.S. diplomats have trouble going outside the Zone for official appointments because of security concerns. The Kirkuk consulate close at the end of July 2012 in part due to security concerns and to save costs.

Ambassador-nominee to Iraq Brett McGurk stated in his June 6, 2012, confirmation hearings that the U.S. Embassy in Baghdad, built at a cost of about $750 million, is too large and carries too much staff relative to the remaining mission. He said the State Department plan is to cut the staff at the embassy by about 25% by the end of 2013. The process of reducing staff in part accounts for the fall in the total number of U.S. personnel in Iraq to about 12,500 from nearly 17,000 at the time of the completion of the U.S. withdrawal at the end of 2011.

As shown in **Table 3** below (in the note), the State Department request for operations (which includes costs for the Embassy as well as other facilities and all personnel in Iraq) is about $2.7 billion for FY2013, down from $3.6 billion requested for FY2012—with FY2012 considered a "transition year" to State Department leadership, and requiring high start-up costs. In addition, press reports say the Central Intelligence Agency is planning to reduce its staff to about 40% of the 700 personnel it had in Iraq at the height of the U.S. military presence there.[40]

The debate over staff is separate from but related to the debate over whether the State Department, using security contractors, can fully secure its personnel in Iraq. A staff report of the Senate Foreign Relations Committee, released January 31, 2011, expressed substantial skepticism.[41] Still, no U.S. civilian personnel in Iraq have been killed or injured since the troop withdrawal.

Status of the Ambassador Post. Another issue is the Ambassador position itself. As noted above, Brett McGurk was nominated and had his Senate confirmation hearings on June 6, 2012. Shortly thereafter, he withdrew after revelations of an extramarital relationship with an Iraq-based U.S. journalist during his prior service at the U.S. Embassy in Baghdad. The Administration subsequently named deputy chief of mission in Iraq, Robert Stephen Beecroft, as Ambassador-Designate. His confirmation hearings were held by the Senate Foreign Relations Committee on September 19, 2012.

---

[39] Tim Arango. "U.S. Plans to Cut Its Staff by Half at Iraq Embassy." *New York Times*, February 8, 2012.

[40] Siobhan Gorman and Adam Entous. "CIA Prepares Iraq Pullback." Wall Street Journal, June 5, 2012.

[41] Senate Foreign Relations Committee. "Iraq: The Transition From a Military Mission to A Civilian-Led Effort." S.Prt. 112-3. January 31, 2011.

Regional Reinforcement Capability

In conjunction with the withdrawal, Defense Secretary Panetta stressed that the United States would retain a large capability in the Persian Gulf region, presumably to be in position to assist the ISF were it to falter, and to demonstrate continuing U.S. interest in Iraq's security as well as to deter Iran. The United States has about 50,000 military personnel in the region, including about 15,000 mostly U.S. Army forces in Kuwait, a portion of which are, as of mid-2012, combat ready rather than purely support forces. There are also about 7,500 mostly Air Force personnel in Qatar; 5,000 mostly Navy personnel in Bahrain; and about 3,000 mostly Air Force and Navy in the UAE, with very small numbers in Saudi Arabia and Oman. The remainder are part of at least one (and often two) aircraft carrier task force in or near the Gulf at any given time. The forces are in the Gulf under defense cooperation agreements with all six Gulf Cooperation Council (GCC) states that give the United States access to their military facilities and, in several cases, to station forces and preposition even heavy armor.

Table 2. March 2010 COR Election: Final, Certified Results by Province

Province	Elected Seats in COR	Results
Baghdad	68	Maliki: 26 seats; Iraqiyya: 24 seats; INA: 17 seats; minority reserved: 2 seats
Nineveh (Mosul)	31	Iraqiiya: 20; Kurdistan Alliance: 8; INA: 1; Accordance: 1; Unity (Bolani): 1; minority reserved: 3
Qadisiyah	11	Maliki: 4; INA: 5; Iraqiyya: 2
Muthanna	7	Maliki: 4; INA: 3
Dohuk	10	Kurdistan Alliance: 9; other Kurdish lists: 1; minority reserved: 1
Basra	24	Maliki: 14 ; INA: 7; Iraqiyya: 3
Anbar	14	Iraqiyya: 11; Unity (Bolani): 1; Accordance: 2
Karbala	10	Maliki: 6; INA: 3; Iraqiyya: 1
Wasit	11	Maliki: 5; INA: 4; Iraqiyya: 2
Dhi Qar	18	Maliki: 8; INA: 9; Iraqiyya: 1
Sulaymaniyah	17	Kurdistan Alliance: 8; other Kurds: 9
Kirkuk (Tamim)	12	Iraqiyya: 6; Kurdistan Alliance: 6
Babil	16	Maliki: 8; INA: 5; Iraqiyya: 3
Irbil	14	Kurdistan Alliance: 10; other Kurds: 4
Najaf	12	Maliki: 7; INA: 5
Diyala	13	Iraqiyya: 8; INA: 3; Maliki: 1; Kurdistan Alliance: 1
Salahuddin	12	Iraqiyya: 8; Unity (Bolani): 2; Accordance: 2
Maysan	10	Maliki: 4; INA: 6
Total Seats	**325** (310 elected + 8 minority reserved + 7 compensatory)	Iraqiyya: 89 + 2 compensatory = 91
		Maliki: 87 + 2 compensatory = 89
		INA: 68 + 2 compensatory = 70 (of which about 40 are Sadrist)
		Kurdistan Alliance: 42 +1 compensatory = 43
		Unity (Bolani): 4
		Accordance: 6
		other Kurdish: 14
		minority reserved: 8

Source: Iraqi Higher Election Commission, March 26, 2010.

Notes: Seat totals are approximate and their exact allocation may be subject to varying interpretations of Iraqi law. Total seat numbers include likely allocations of compensatory seats. Total seats do not add to 325 total seats in the COR due to some uncertainties in allocations.

Table 3. U.S. Assistance to Iraq: FY2003-FY2013

(appropriations/allocations in millions of $)

	FY '03	04	05	06	07	08	09	10	11	12	Total 03-12	FY'13 Request
IRRF	2,475	18,389	—	10	—	—	—	—	—	—	20,874	
ESF	—	—	—	1,535.4	1,677	429	541.5	382.5	325.7	299	5,190	262.9
Democracy Fund	—	—	—	—	250	75	—	—	—	—	325	
IFTA (Treasury Dept. Asst.)	—	—	—	13.0	2.8	—	—	—	—	—	15.8	
NADR	—	—	3.6	—	18.4	20.4	35.5	30.3	29.8	32	170	30.3
Refugee Accounts (MRA and ERMA)	39.6	.1	—	—	78.3	278	260	316	280	—	1,252	
IDA	22	—	7.1	.3	45	85	51	42	17	—	269	
Other USAID Funds	470	—	—	—	—	23.8	—	—	—	—	494	
INCLE	—	—	—	91.4	170	85	20	702	114.6	500	1,683	850
FMF	—	—	—	—	—	—	—	—	—	850	850	900
IMET	—	1.2	—	—	1.1	—	2	2	1.7	2	10	2
DOD—ISF Funding	—	—	5,391	3,007	5,542	3,000	1,000	1,000	1,500	—	20,440	
DOD—Iraq Army	51.2	—	210	—	—	—	—	—	—	—	261	
DOD—CERP	—	140	718	708	750	996	339	263	44.0	—	3,958	
DOD—Oil Repair	802	—	—	—	—	—	—	—	—	—	802	
DOD—Business Support	—	—	—	—	50.0	50.0	74.0	—	—	—	174	
Total	**3,859**	**18,548**	**6,329**	**5,365**	**8,584**	**5,042**	**2,323**	**2,738**	**2,313**	**1,683**	**56,768**	**2,045.2**

Sources: State Department FY2013 Executive Budget Summary, February 2012; SIGIR Report to Congress, January 30, 2012; and CRS calculations. FY2012 appropriations in Consolidated Appropriation, P.L. 112-74.

Notes: Table prepared by Curt Tarnoff, Specialist in Foreign Affairs, on February 17, 2012. This table does not contain agency operational costs, including CPA, State Department, and PRTs, except where these are embedded in the larger reconstruction accounts. Estimated operational costs to date are an additional $9.3 billion, including $3.6 billion estimated for FY2012. Approximately $2.7 billion is requested by State Department for these costs in FY2013. Possible cuts in staff at the U.S. embassy and other locations is addressed in this report. IG oversight costs estimated at $417 million. IMET=International Military Education and Training; IRRF=Iraq Relief and Reconstruction Fund; INCLE=International Narcotics and Law Enforcement Fund; ISF=Iraq Security Force; NADR=Nonproliferation, Anti-Terrorism, Demining and Related: ESF=Economic Support Fund; IDA=International Disaster Assistance; FMF=Foreign Military Financing; ISF= Iraqi Security Forces.

Table 4. Recent Democracy Assistance to Iraq

(in millions of current $)

	FY2009	FY2010 (act.)	FY2011	FY2012
Rule of Law and Human Rights	32.45	33.3	16.5	29.75
Good Governance	143.64	117.40	90.33	100.5
Political Competition/Consensus-Building	41.00	52.60	30.00	16.25
Civil Society	87.53	83.6	32.5	55.5
Totals	**304.62**	**286.9**	**169.33**	**202.0**

Source: Congressional Budget Justification, March 2011. Figures for these accounts are included in the overall assistance figures presented in the table above.

Table 5. January 31, 2009, Provincial Election Results (Major Slates)

Baghdad—55 regular seats, plus one Sabean and one Christian set-aside seat	State of Law (Maliki)—38% (28 seats); Independent Liberals Trend (pro-Sadr)—9% (5 seats); Accord Front (Sunni mainstream)—9% (9 seats); Iraq National (Allawi)—8.6%; Shahid Mihrab and Independent Forces (ISCI)—5.4% (3 seats) ; National Reform list (of former P.M. Ibrahim al-Jafari)—4.3% (3 seats)
Basra—34 regular seats, plus one Christian seat	State of Law—37% (20); ISCI—11.6% (5); Sadr—5% (2); Fadhila (previously dominant in Basra)—3.2% (0); Allawi—3.2% (0); Jafari list—2.5% (0). Governor : Shiltagh Abbud (Maliki list); Council chair: Jabbar Amin (Maliki list)
Nineveh—34 regular seats, plus one set aside each for Shabaks, Yazidis, and Christians	Hadbaa—48.4%; Fraternal Nineveh—25.5%; IIP—6.7%; Hadbaa took control of provincial council and administration. Governor is Atheel al-Nujaifi (Hadbaa).
Najaf—28 seats	State of Law—16.2% (7); ISCI—14.8% (7); Sadr—12.2% (6); Jafari—7% (2); Allawi—1.8% (0); Fadhila—1.6% (0). Council chairman: Maliki list
Babil—30 seats	State of Law—12.5% (8); ISCI—8.2% (5); Sadr—6.2% (3); Jafari—4.4% (3); Allawi—3.4%; Accord Front—2.3% (3); Fadhila—1.3%. New Council chair: Kadim Majid Tuman (Sadrist); Governor—Salman Zirkani (Maliki list)
Diyala—29 seats	Accord Front list—21.1%; Kurdistan Alliance—17.2%; Allawi—9.5%; State of Law—6 %. New council leans heavily Accord, but allied with Kurds and ISCI.
Muthanna—26 seats	State of Law—10.9% (5); ISCI—9.3% (5); Jafari—6.3% (3); Sadr—5.5% (2); Fadhila—3.7%.
Anbar—29 seats	Iraq Awakening (Sahawa-Sunni tribals)—18%; National Iraqi Project Gathering (established Sunni parties, excluding IIP)—17.6%;; Allawi—6.6%; Tribes of Iraq—4.5%.
Maysan—27 seats	State of Law—17.7% (8); ISCI—14.6% (8); Sadr—7; Jafari—8.7% (4); Fadhila—3.2%; Allawi—2.3%. New Governor: Mohammad al-Sudani (Maliki); Council chair: Hezbollah Iraq
Dhi Qar—31 seats	State of Law—23.1% (13); pro-Sadr—14.1% (7); ISCI—11.1% (5); Jafari—7.6% (4); Fadhila—6.1%; Allawi—2.8%. Governor—Maliki list; Council chair: Sadrist
Karbala—27 seats	List of Maj. Gen. Yusuf al-Habbubi (Saddam-era local official)—13.3% (1 seat); State of Law—8.5% (9); Sadr—6.8% (4); ISCI—6.4% (4); Jafari—2.5% ; Fadhila—2.5%.
Salah Ad Din—28 seats	IIP-led list—14.5%; Allawi—13.9%; Sunni list without IIP—8.7%; State of Law—3.5%; ISCI—2.9%. Council leans Accord/IIP
Qadissiyah—28 seats	State of Law—23.1% (11); ISCI—11.7% (5); Jafari—8.2% (3); Allawi—8%; Sadr—6.7% (2); Fadhila—4.1%. New governor: Salim Husayn (Maliki list)
Wasit—28 seats	State of Law—15.3% (13); ISCI—10% (6); Sadr—6% (3); Allawi—4.6%; Fadhila—2.7%. Governor: Shiite independent; Council chair: ISCI

Source: UNAMI translation of results issued February 2, 2009, by the Independent Higher Election Commission of Iraq; Vissar, Reidar. The Provincial Elections: The Seat Allocation Is Official and the Coalition-Forming Process Begins. February 19, 2009.

Table 6. Election Results (January and December 2005)

Bloc/Party	Seats (Jan. 05)	Seats (Dec. 05)
United Iraqi Alliance (UIA, Shiite Islamist). 85 seats after departure of Fadilah (15 seats) and Sadr faction (28 seats) in 2007. Islamic Supreme Council of Iraq of Abd al-Aziz al-Hakim has 30; Da'wa Party (25 total: Maliki faction, 12, and Anizi faction, 13); independents (30).	140	128
Kurdistan Alliance—KDP (24); PUK (22); independents (7)	75	53
Iraqis List (secular, Allawi); added Communist and other mostly Sunni parties for Dec. vote.	40	25
Iraq Accord Front. Main Sunni bloc; not in Jan. vote. Consists of Iraqi Islamic Party (IIP, Tariq al-Hashimi, 26 seats); National Dialogue Council of Khalaf Ulayyan (7); General People's Congress of Adnan al-Dulaymi (7); independents (4).	—	44
National Iraqi Dialogue Front (Sunni, led by former Baathist Saleh al-Mutlak) Not in Jan. 2005 vote.	—	11
Kurdistan Islamic Group (Islamist Kurd) (votes with Kurdistan Alliance)	2	5
Iraqi National Congress (Chalabi). Was part of UIA list in Jan. 05 vote	—	0
Iraqis Party (Yawar, Sunni); Part of Allawi list in Dec. vote	5	—
Iraqi Turkomen Front (Turkomen, Kirkuk-based, pro-Turkey)	3	1
National Independent and Elites (Jan)/Risalyun (Message, Dec) pro-Sadr	3	2
People's Union (Communist, non-sectarian); on Allawi list in Dec. vote	2	—
Islamic Action (Shiite Islamist, Karbala)	2	0
National Democratic Alliance (non-sectarian, secular)	1	—
Rafidain National List (Assyrian Christian)	1	1
Liberation and Reconciliation Gathering (Umar al-Jabburi, Sunni, secular)	1	3
Ummah (Nation) Party. (Secular, Mithal al-Alusi, former INC activist)	0	1
Yazidi list (small Kurdish, heterodox religious minority in northern Iraq)	—	1

Notes: Number of polling places: January: 5,200; December: 6,200; Eligible voters: 14 million in January election; 15 million in October referendum and December; Turnout: January: 58% (8.5 million votes)/ October: 66% (10 million)/December: 75% (12 million).

Table 7. Assessments of the Benchmarks

Benchmark	July 12, 2007, Admin. Report	GAO (Sept. 07)	Sept. 14, 2007, Admin. Report	Subsequent Actions and Assessments—May 2008 Administration report, June 2008 GAO report, International Compact with Iraq Review in June 2008, and U.S. Embassy Weekly Status Reports (and various press sources)
1. Forming Constitutional Review Committee (CRC) and completing review	(S) satisfactory	unmet	S	CRC filed final report in August 2008 but major issues remain unresolved and require achievement of consensus among major faction leaders.
2. Enacting and implementing laws on De-Baathification	(U) unsatisfact.	unmet	S	"Justice and Accountability Law" passed Jan. 12, 2008. Allows about 30,000 fourth ranking Baathists to regain their jobs, and 3,500 Baathists in top three party ranks would receive pensions. Could allow for judicial prosecution of all ex-Baathists and bars ex-Saddam security personnel from regaining jobs. De-Baathification officials used this law to try to harm the prospects of rivals in March 2010 elections.
3. Enacting and implementing oil laws that ensure equitable distribution of resources	U	unmet	U	Framework and three implementing laws long stalled over KRG-central government disputes, but draft legislation still pending in COR. Revenue being distributed equitably, including 17% revenue for KRG. Kurds also getting that share of oil exported from fields in KRG area.
4. Enacting and implementing laws to form semi-autonomous regions	S	partly met	S	Regions law passed October 2006, with relatively low threshold (petition by 33% of provincial council members) to start process to form new regions, took effect April 2008. November 2008: petition by 2% of Basra residents submitted to IHEC (another way to start forming a region) to convert Basra province into a single province "region. Signatures of 8% more were required by mid-January 2009; not achieved. Najaf, Diyala, Salahuddin, and Anbar have asked for a referendum to become a region.
5. Enacting and implementing: (a) a law to establish a higher electoral commission, (b) provincial elections law; (c) a law to specify authorities of provincial bodies, and (d) set a date for provincial elections	S on (a) and U on the others	overall unmet; (a) met	S on (a) and (c)	Draft law stipulating powers of provincial governments adopted February 13, 2008, took effect April 2008. Implementing election law adopted September 24, 2008, provided for provincial elections by January 31, 2009. Those elections were held, as discussed above.
6. Enacting and implementing legislation addressing amnesty for former insurgents	no rating	unmet	Same as July	Law to amnesty "non-terrorists" among 25,000 Iraq-held detainees passed February 13, 2008. Most of these have been released. 19,000 detainees held by U.S. were transferred to Iraqi control under SA.
7. Enacting and implementing laws on militia disarmament	no rating	unmet	Same as July	March 2008 Basra operation, discussed above, viewed as move against militias. On April 9, 2008, Maliki demanded all militias disband as condition for their parties to participate in provincial elections. Law on militia demobilization stalled.
8. Establishing political, media, economic, and services committee to	S	met	met	No longer applicable; U.S. "surge" has ended and U.S. troops now out of Iraq.

Benchmark	July 12, 2007, Admin. Report	GAO (Sept. 07)	Sept. 14, 2007, Admin. Report	Subsequent Actions and Assessments—May 2008 Administration report, June 2008 GAO report, International Compact with Iraq Review in June 2008, and U.S. Embassy Weekly Status Reports (and various press sources)
support U.S. "surge"				
9. Providing three trained and ready brigades to support U.S. surge	S	partly met	S	No longer applicable. Eight brigades were assigned to assist the surge when it was in operation.
10. Providing Iraqi commanders with authorities to make decisions, without political intervention, to pursue all extremists, including Sunni insurgents and Shiite militias	U	unmet	S to pursue extremists U on political interference	No significant change. Still some U.S. concern over the Office of the Commander in Chief (part of Maliki's office) control over appointments to the ISF—favoring Shiites. Some politically motivated leaders remain in ISF. But, National Police said to include more Sunnis in command jobs and rank and file than one year ago.
11. Ensuring Iraqi Security Forces (ISF) providing even-handed enforcement of law	U	unmet	S on military, U on police	U.S. interpreted March 2008 Basra operation as effort by Maliki to enforce law even-handedly. Widespread Iraqi public complaints of politically-motivated administration of justice.
12. Ensuring that the surge plan in Baghdad will not provide a safe haven for any outlaw, no matter the sect	S	partly met	S	No longer applicable with end of surge. Ethno-sectarian violence has fallen sharply in Baghdad.
13. (a) Reducing sectarian violence and (b) eliminating militia control of local security	Mixed. S on (a); U on (b)	unmet	same as July 12	Sectarian violence has not re-accelerated outright, although there are fears the political crisis in December 2011 could reignite sectarian conflict.
14. Establishing Baghdad joint security stations	S	met	S	Over 50 joint security stations operated in Baghdad at the height of U.S. troop surge. Closed in compliance with June 30, 2009, U.S. pull out from the cities.
15. Increasing ISF units capable of operating independently	U	unmet	U	ISF now securing Iraq under the SA. Iraqi Air Force not likely to be able to secure airspace and DOD has approved potential sale to Iraq of F-16s and other major equipment.
16. Ensuring protection of minority parties in COR	S	met	S	No change. Rights of minority parties protected by Article 37 of constitution. Minorities given a minimum seat allocated in 2010 election law.
17. Allocating and spending $10 billion in 2007 capital budget for reconstruction.	S	partly met	S	About 63% of the $10 billion 2007 allocation for capital projects was spent.
18. Ensuring that Iraqi authorities not falsely accusing ISF members	U	unmet	U	Some governmental recriminations against some ISF officers still observed.

Source: Compiled by CRS.

Author Contact Information

Kenneth Katzman
Specialist in Middle Eastern Affairs
kkatzman@crs.loc.gov, 7-7612